Editorial

On 19 March I attended a performance of Bizet's *Carmen* at the Buxton Opera House. The Opera House makes any event special – gilds it, as it were – even when one is sitting at the very edge of the second circle with the hot lights half-obscuring the half-view of the left-hand side of the stage. What made the event even more special was that the production was by the Dnipro Opera from Ukraine, with a large cast and a 30-piece orchestra. Their travels, by large coach in which it is said they spend their nights, took them to various small cities around England where they performed *Madama Butterfly* and *Aida* as well as *Carmen*. Buxton was sold out and full of yellow and blue. At the end it erupted into flags and a resounding rendition of the Ukrainian National Anthem, a tune which is becoming quite familiar in our public spaces. Our rendition was so loud and spirited that perhaps an echo of it reached Kyiv and Odessa.

Neither Carmen herself nor Don Jose seemed to have stinted on the varenyky or holubtsi. Carmen had a rich, blurry voice, but it was impossible not be drawn in to the star-crossed drama. The orchestra was precise, brisk and well conducted. I wondered what it must feel like to be in a touring national opera company when, back home, your nation is being bombed and shredded. How do you spend your days, do you see yourself and your art as somehow in service of a national cause? The soldiers, drinkers and peasants all looked as though they were of military age.

I wondered, too, what was happening to the wider Ukrainian culture back at home. Certainly the publishing news in the United Kingdom and United States has been alive to the damage the war has done to Ukrainian bookselling, book-making and writing. The one publishing dividend of the war has been the enormous growth in international awareness of what Ukrainian culture includes, and in translations from Ukrainian into the other languages of Europe. Rights sales of Ukrainian books rose from 120 in 2021 to 230 in 2022.

Ukrainian publishers, writers and booksellers have been featured at book festivals all over Europe, and in public galleries some works previously described as 'Russian' are being re-labelled 'Ukrainian', even as the Russian troops cart off the contents of distinguished large and small Ukrainian museums and galleries to Russia as spoils of war. This may seem at present a small matter compared with the number of civilian deaths and injuries and military deaths and injuries on both sides, the millions of exiles created, the appalling reversal of a prosperous and largely peaceful culture. In the longer term the cultural damage will be differently calculated: 'citizens of a world/shared in shards', as Oksana Maksymchuk wrote in her poem 'Stolen Time' (*PNR* 268).

On 17 March *Publishers Weekly* reported on the consequences of the Russian invasion on Ukrainian publishing one year into the war. The immediate occasion was that, at the Bologna Book Fair earlier in March, Old Lion Publishing House (Lviv) had been chosen as European children's publisher of the year.

In twelve war-torn months, new titles published in Ukraine fell to almost half the level of the previous year, from 17,000 to under 9,000. It is not hard to imagine how the printing sector has fared with the targeted and stray bombings, the damage to infrastructure and the curtailment of imports. In 2021 25.7 million books were printed; only 9.2 million last year. *Publisher's Weekly* reports Yulia

Orlova, CEO of Vivat Publishing in Kharkiv, the second-largest publisher in the country, as saying, 'Ukraine would import 60,000 tons of paper in a typical year; however in 2022, the industry only received 20,000 tons.' *PW* also reported, 'In the two years prior to the war, the Translate Ukraine program, run by UBI, offered €300,000 to support the translation of Ukrainian works, resulting in 113 books published in 24 countries. The program was halted when the war started, but UBI announced that it will restart soon, with the aim of supporting the translation of 50 more books.'

Publishing, like the rest of the economy in Ukraine, does somehow – after the trauma of the invasion and a period of adjustment – continue. 'Vivat [...] shut down when the war started, as many of its staff of 100 were forced to relocate and work remotely. After shipping 20 truckloads of books to western Ukraine, it began fulfilling book orders in April. In June, it resumed publishing new titles, releasing 350 last year – a small drop from the nearly 400 published in 2021. In addition, Vivat opened a new bookstore in Kyiv in October.' Other companies uprooted themselves, or relocated staff abroad. It is hoped that the main book festivals may return to business soon and that the world, so keenly interested in Ukraine now, will not forget it as the war drags on and its consequences are felt with increasing pain in hitherto supportive countries.

An Austrian friend wrote to me on 23 March to say she and her husband had been watching a DVD by a German volunteer soldier in Ukraine but had had to turn it off, the young man's 'self-assurance and pride' had become unbearable. I wondered why. 'He was pro-Donbass, pro-Putin.' It had not occurred to me that volunteers might take such a course. 'On that tableland scored by rivers, / Our thoughts have bodies; the menacing shapes of our fever / Are precise and alive.' It is a division equivalent to the one that split volunteers – including the English – at the time of the Spanish Civil War, which so roused Auden and his contemporaries. Some of the causes of division were analogous. They had to do with religious dogma, the end of empire, an acute nostalgia for a simpler ideological order and a truth dictated, not found. The literature from that Civil War remains instructive and memorable; the literature emerging from the current conflict may prove equally so. Depending on the outcomes.

Letters to the editor

Martin Caseley writes: Poetry should not necessarily require explanatory footnotes. A bad example might be Eliot's original notes to 'The Waste Land', originally supplied to bulk out the book, rather than aid the reader. Nevertheless, having read and enjoyed Joseph Minden's 'Headstones' sequence in *PN Review 268*, I feel compelled to offer one to aid readers.

Whilst references to Tyne Cot, Portland stone, Poperinge and other WWI battlefields can be worked out, the casual reader may be flummoxed by 'Reality Checkpoint', referenced in the final section. Anyone who has ever lived in Cambridge, however, would notice Parker's Piece also mentioned. This square green space at the north end of Mill Road, is on the 'alternative' side of the city, not far from what used to be Cambridge College of Arts and Technology: in the middle of this popular open space, where two footpaths cross, there stands one flamboyantly-carved cast-iron lampost, identified by graffiti as 'Reality Checkpoint' in whose 'lemony glow' (in Minden's phrase) many, including this writer, have stood and walked over the years.

The name may refer to the idea of those from the University entering the 'real world' if they proceed any further towards the Mill Road area, and it has become a well-known local landmark with its own informative Wikipedia page. It is not simply metaphor: the unofficial name has been painted over and renewed several times over the years.

Anthony Barnett writes: A Basil Bunting anecdote, funny at the time. While working at the Better Books New Compton Street store in the mid 1960s an opportunity arose to go for lunch with Bunting. I asked many innocent or ignorant or both questions, among which, what did Bunting think of e. e. cummings? 'I don't know whether he is coming or going,' he replied.

Mark Dow wrote to Five Dials, *to which he had contributed in 2011, to ask whether he could submit again. He received this reply dated 7 February 2023.*

'Hi Mark - lovely to hear from you and apologies for the

delayed reply! We've been on winter hiatus. Since 2011 we have changed our editorial focus to publishing early career writers from underrepresented communities (eg POC, queer, working class, disabled). If this applies to you, great! Do shoot me over your pieces at [e-dress] and one of us will come back to you with our thoughts. If not, I'm sure the pieces will find good homes at other publications, I'm sorry we're not the right space for them. All good wishes, Hermione'

He replied, "Hi Hermione - It's disappointing to hear the formulaic categorizations from Five Dials but thank you for replying. Mark'

News & Notes

Scully • *John McAuliffe writes:* Irish poet Maurice Scully died in Bolea, Spain on 5 March 2023. Scully published pamphlets and extracts from serial work with a roll-call of small presses, including Raven Arts, Galloping Dog Press, etruscan books, Poetical Histories, Wild Honey Press, Pig Press, hardPressed poetry, Smithereens and Reality Street Editions, with larger collected editions published by Dedalus Press and most recently Shearsman, *Things That Happen*. Scully's modernist, observational work was compared to William Carlos Williams' *Paterson* and often read alongside peers including Trevor Joyce, Catherine Walsh and Randolph Healy, poets who were also involved, as he was, in small press and magazine editing. In Ireland, he was awarded the Macaulay Fellowship in 1981 and Arts Council Bursaries in Literature in 1986 & 1988 along with the Katherine & Patrick Kavanagh Fellowship in 2004. He was elected to the Irish state's artists association, Aosdána, in 2009.

Verlaine • *Martin Caseley writes:* Tom Verlaine, who died in January aged seventy-three after a short illness, was one of a small group of young, bohemian performers who brought a new poetic sensibility into the world of rock music when new wave exploded in the mid-1970s. Together with his close friend – and former partner – Patti Smith, he expanded rock lyrics to include influences from the writers they loved, French symbolists Rimbaud and Verlaine, noir pulp novelists such as Raymond Chandler and Beat iconoclasts such as William Burroughs and Allen Ginsberg. Primarily, however, Verlaine became known for his scorching, Coltrane-inspired, arpeggiated lead guitar playing, which could be tender, brutal and asymmetrical in turn. When Patti Smith moved from poetry readings into music, Verlaine's guitar was all over her debut 1974 single *Piss Factory/Hey Joe*, on the latter song managing to make the listener forget all about Jimi Hendrix's defining version. He was also involved in two of the most epochal albums of the 1970s, Patti Smith's *Horses* (1975) and, two years later, his own band Television's *Marquee Moon*, a record regularly cited as an instant classic, which became hugely influential on later bands such as REM. The lyrics for Television songs were opaque, stream-of-conscious screeds of symbols, memories, anecdotes and joky streetwise slang, often difficult to interpret due to Verlaine's strange accentuation and idiosyncratic delivery. The song 'Marquee Moon', for example, begins 'I remember how the darkness doubled/ I recall lightning struck itself', staking out new territory in its self-cancelling metaphors. Lou Reed had used street slang in American rock before and Dylan had mixed influences from the Beats and Lenny Bruce into some of his crucial mid-60s songs, but Tom Verlaine made this approach vital and dynamic to a new generation of discerning listeners by allying it to a handful of superb songs, nearly all of which can be heard on *Marquee Moon*, sounding as vital, energised and powerful now as the day they were recorded.

'Propaganda' • *Christine Blackwell alerted us to the following from the* Moscow Times *of 10 January.* Ordinary Russians are unable to access an increasingly broad range of literature as bookshops and libraries pull titles from their shelves amid a wartime crackdown on political dissent and a November law banning LGBT 'propaganda'. In particular, failing to comply with the controversial — and vague — anti-LGBT law puts shops at risk of large fines or, at worst, closure.

'We are actually afraid,' said Lyubov Belyatskaya, co-owner of Vse Svobodny, an independent, liberal-leaning bookstore in St. Petersburg. The problems faced by bookshops and libraries, which were previously places less affected by Russia's political repression, are a testament to the mounting pressure on the world of literature that is narrowing access to both fiction and non-fiction titles.

A lack of clarity about the anti-LGBT law signed by President Vladimir Putin late in 2022 — which outlaws public depictions of 'non-traditional' relationships — has created confusion among booksellers about which titles can now be legally displayed and sold.

'Everyone started panicking,' said the owner of another liberal-leaning bookstore in St. Petersburg who asked to remain anonymous. 'Some of our vendors stopped supplying some books on their own initiative even though they weren't really covered by the new law.'

Representatives from several retailers told the *Moscow Times* that they had received no information from the authorities about which books were prohibited. As a result, some shops are removing titles on their own initiative or in line with requests from publishers. Others are consulting with lawyers. [...] Some businesses have taken a blanket approach, pulling books with even a passing mention of LGBT relationships or lifestyles. ...

'It's very simple: we have a list coming from the city administration and we comply with it," a shop administrator at the Bukvoyed bookstore in the center of St.

Petersburg told a *Moscow Times* reporter on a recent visit. 'It will work just like with forbidden literature, such as *Mein Kampf*.' LitRes, Russia's largest e-book seller, has even asked some authors to rewrite works to comply with the anti-LGBT law, the RBC news website reported in December.

Joan Margarit Award • In March the Spanish newspaper *El Pais* announced the birth of the new annual international Joan Margarit Award for Poetry, an initiative of the invaluable Instituto Cervantes and the publishing house La Cama Sol. The purse is a significant one in the poetry world, worth 7,000 Euros. Poets will be translated into Spanish, English and French. The eponymous poet wrote in Catalan and Spanish, and translated Hardy, Rilke and Elizabeth Bishop, among others, into his languages.

Bollingen Prize • Joy Harjo was awarded the 2023 Bollingen Prize for American Poetry. The prize has honoured fifty-three poets, including Harjo, among them W. H. Auden, Marianne Moore, Wallace Stevens, Louise Bogan, Léonie Adams, Robert Frost, Susan Howe, Charles Wright, Louise Glück, Nathaniel Mackey, Jean Valentine, Charles Bernstein, and Mei-mei Berssenbrugge. This year's judges include Berssenbrugge, Natalie Diaz, and Ilya Kaminsky. The book they celebrate is entitled *Weaving Sundown in a Scarlet Light: Fifty Poems for Fifty Years* and for her lifetime achievement in and contributions to American poetry. In this case the purse is ample, $175,000. 'Poetry has been my most challenging teacher and the most rewarding,' Harjo declared with feeling. Among other honours, she has been poet laureate of the United States for three terms (2019–2022) and has received the National Book Critics Circle Ivan Sandrof Lifetime Achievement Award, the Ruth Lilly Prize for Lifetime Achievement from the Poetry Foundation, the Academy of American Poets Wallace Stevens Award, and a Guggenheim Fellowship. She is the editor of *Living Nations, Living Words: An Anthology of First Peoples Poetry*, a legacy of her poet laureate project. She is a chancellor of the Academy of American Poets, Board Chair of the Native Arts and Cultures Foundation, and the first artist-in-residence for the Bob Dylan Center in Tulsa, Oklahoma, where she lives.

Poet of the Ordinary • The American poet Linda Pastan has died at the age of ninety. Reviewing her *New and Selected Poems* in these pages in 1999 (*PNR* 130), Ian Tromp wrote, '*Carnival Evening* gives a very good introduction to [her] work. She is an important poet; for the quiet precision of her voice alone, she deserves to be read. Some of her poems of domestic grief - even some of those of matrimonial grievance - are remarkably moving. In her most successful poems, Pastan's delicate use of form and her careful attention to internal rhythm, her ear well tuned to sounds and to silence, ensure that "language does the best it can".' She was a 'poet of the ordinary' – and much more.

Neruda's Death • The cause of Pablo Neruda's death in 1973 was officially given as cancer. Suddenly he has had a second going, with long-familiar stories that he was in fact murdered re-surfacing and gaining some credence. The rumour began in 2011 when his quondam chauffeur alleged that he had been injected in the stomach shortly before he died. He was preparing to go into exile in Mexico, the left-wing government which he supported having been toppled a few days before.

Many men who suffer from prostate cancer have hormone injections in the stomach. This was not a sufficient explanation and the rumour gained traction. A decade-long investigation was initiated. At last, 'a team of international forensic experts gave a Chilean judge their final report about their analysis of Mr. Neruda's exhumed remains.' The mystery remains intact: the forensic experts were not unanimous. Their verdict was 'maybe, maybe not'.

Reports

Touch and Mourning

Part 4: Meeting the Author

ANTHONY VAHNI CAPILDEO

The generation above me is dying. It is wrong to notice this. Younger death is news that no longer stays news. The political clock runs backwards, and the pandemic clock has been stopped. However, the generation above me is passing. It is like breathing thin air that does not refresh; like staring into a moving lift shaft. Why am I not writing elegies? Is it because so many of those poets turned people into bodies? With a look, a gesture, a refusal of a life-changing reference, an inexhaustible demand – O Muse – for our unpaid words. Touch is not immediate; it lives on replay in the bodymind. Tact is not only about the unknowability of others; it enables the refusal to know. The skin is not a container; the sense of self can split, dissolve, or multiply. My words would mourn; but my body recalls the touches.

Imagine meeting a legendary poet for the first time. He does a lot of listening to you and your friend. His facial expressions show a sincere practice of humility and wonder. Apropos of nothing, he leans forward. 'I want to be your agent!' he barks. He leans back wistfully. Uncomfortably, you laugh it off: 'But...you're not an agent? I don't need an agent...What does an agent do?' As if automated, he leans forward and barks again. He will not take no for an answer. At some point, he gazes into your eyes. It would be impolite, but his right to intensity has been established. The humility and wonder return. 'You have oval pupils!' he exclaims. *No, no I don't*. 'Like an animal,' he says. 'I've never seen that before in a human being.' *Can I disagree?* 'They're oval, like an animal's,' he concludes, sincerely. It seems that you have agreed to something.

'Animal imagery', as they used to say in school. You have read *Othello*. You have not yet read Zora Neale Hurston. You do not have a shapeshifter's powers. What animal?

When he is gone, as in dead and gone, you have avoided speaking to him for years. He is Falstaffian, hard to think of funereally. You compulsively remember the night he thrust himself at you, saying, 'I am not a good man! I am not a good man!', after you trust his mentorship enough to ask for help with an abusive situation. You stayed clothed, and left ungratefully; and now he is gone, as in gone for good, you feel that you have betrayed him all round -- by not reaching out to those who mourn him; by asking for money for writing work, in your separate and new writerly life; by not being an animal in his imaginary, or menagerie.

Fled touch and baffled mourning, as an anti-creative prompt: curse or elegy?

Confessional? Confusion. In Puccini's opera, *Tosca*, the artist Cavaradossi sings about how his lover has dark eyes, whereas another woman inspiring his painting has blue eyes, but the mystery of art reconciles the differing beauties into one composite muse – 'l'arte nel suo mistero / Le diverse bellezze insiem confonde'. *Confondere* is a 'false friend', similar-looking but not quite equivalent to the English 'confound'; not quite 'confuse', 'mix', 'mingle', or 'interchange'. As a failed Inspirational Object, you know that there is another side to this *confonder(si)*. Another kind of aggregation may occur, this time in the mind of the one who is being turned into a body.

Traumatic memory can operate creatively, like a collage artist. It snips, pastes, flips inside-out, and assembles its own poetics from the body of the canon – raises a gloriously out-of-place poetics. It is less controllable, and stronger, than a reading strategy for finding resistance, or recreation. When I look into my mind as a writer, not a critic, I find an entirely different recall system at play.

For example: Sylvia Plath's 'Lady Lazarus', a countdown-of-death poem, comes to mind with the volume up on its fiery call to survival. Gerald Manley Hopkins's language is springy. It can go rogue. He and Plath are on your side. For example: Hopkins's 'Spring and Fall', tenderly, if gloomily, telling a young child 'It is Margaret you mourn for', becomes a motto to carry into battle. You are nothing like as pure as Margaret, but when you meet one of those superior word-magicians who would make you into a body while still alive, you have a phrase to condense a lifetime of mourning into the moment you *will not* be bodied, and unselved. For example: the rhythms of Plath's 'Daddy' stick and play lines on repeat, so you can keep track of the changing face of the poet seeking power over you.

> Every woman adores a Fascist,
> The boot in the face, the brute
> Brute heart of a brute like you.

Her poem takes the speaker 'through'. It doesn't have to take you. The brevity and repetition let you stay intentionally in between the poem's spaces. Charm or chant. It witnesses with you. It places the adoring everywoman alongside you, a not-you. That imaginary figure, menagerie figure, absorbs attacks, the way a wooden quintain takes the hits in jousting. The you that you refuse.

If you do not comply with being touched (sympathetic) or tactile (desirable), the consequences need not be bodily fearful. No cause for complaint from you. You simply may, while alive, have your elegy written. People will send you poems addressed to the person they thought you would be for them, sometimes along with an email or cover note expressing disappointment in prose. You are invited to mourn yourself in a form of words of their choosing, having deprived your body of being available to their creativity. If you are not Galatea, a warm statue, ideally with an on and off switch, you will make the most beautiful ruin. You exist sepulchrally, in the historical tour of someone else's personal citadel. You may hear indirectly that there is cause to lament you; perhaps in a prize-winning book, or a cult pamphlet passed amongst your 'allies', probably not titled *This could be us but you playin* or *You're missing out on life*. Invitations may dry up somewhat. Odd looks, or hard words, may come your way at poetic gatherings. There are jobs you don't apply for; teams you fear your friends working with. Your life also serves in the wake of Elegies to the Inspirational Object you Failed to Be.

If you think you do not know anyone like this, think again.

Imagine walking to a market to meet a poet. His deferential tone buzzes close in your ear. You startle, and half-turn. His face, like a ravaged moon not of your planet, has propelled itself out of orbit, on a collision course for a kiss-mistake. You deflect it. Walking in the market square becomes like ice-skating on a rink: leaning to one side, aware that if you fall, other people have blades, and may not be able to stop themselves. Is a hand on your back a hand on your bra strap or just a hand, since your bra strap is on your back? All is well. This was mild. Even if you panic-bought a kilo or two of rhubarb and a brown bag of chanterelles, in a bid to escape politely, nothing happened.

Time will pass. Your elegy will arrive.

You are to have no words.

My words are not in my sword.

Traumatic memory collage artist, what will you make of this? I look into my foolish writer-mind. It presents me with a tumble of ribbons and flowers. For example, Thomas Campion:

There is a garden in her face
Where roses and white lilies grow

He sings to critique the lass who apparently does not cry 'cherry ripe' readily enough. You're beautiful, blooming, why not consumable? This is not at all suitable! Alongside Thomas Campion, memory presents a description of Vivien Leigh's Lavinia, scarlet ribbons at her wrists and mouth representing how her hands have been cut off and her tongue cut out, in *Titus Andronicus*. A pretty flutter, not a gore fest. Then something that does not exist: Hamlet, the son who complains of being too much in the sun, arms heaped with flowers, dressed more prettily than Ophelia. Imagine a tradition of Hamlet being floral with a happy Ophelia! New modes of living into writing. We would not have to die in words, words, words.

Disbelief

ANDY CROFT

Last June the Leningrad-born Canadian translator Maria Bloshteyn contacted me regarding the Kopilka (Piggy Bank) Project, a massive online collection of Russophone poems written about – and against – the war in Ukraine, put together by poets and translators from all over the world (including many still living inside Russia).

Maria was the editor and main translator of Smokestack's big bilingual anthology *Russia is Burning: Poems of the Great Patriotic War,* published in 2020 to mark the seventy-fifth anniversary of the end of the war. She and the other Kopilka translators were looking for a publisher for a bilingual selection of poems about this new and very different war. I immediately offered to publish the book at Smokestack.

Smokestack's list includes bilingual selections by a number of major Russian/Soviet poets from the Second World War – notably Simonov, Tvardovsky and Berggolts (next year Smokestack is publishing a selection of poems by Ilya Ehrenberg). Putting the Kopilka poets into print was a way of honouring those poets and the cause for which they fought. As Tatiana Voltskaya has written, 'We'll get what we deserve, and more. / Unholy war / Has tarnished grandad's medals.'

Whatever arguments there may be about NATO expansion and Ukrainian nationalism, there can be no justification for a war that has left millions displaced and tens of thousands dead or imprisoned, triggered an international economic crisis, turned Russia into a pariah state and the Russian language into a tool of cultural erasure and oppression.

Since the start of the war, the Kremlin has been promoting 'Z-Poetry' glorifying the achievements of the Russian military in the Ukraine. The Russian Ministry of Defence organises poetry competitions and poetry readings. The Russian Union of Writers has published several pro-war anthologies of poetry.

The Kopilka poets are attempting to contest this Kremlin-defined Russophone cultural space in which it is illegal to call the war a 'war' (and not a 'special military operation') and where poets who oppose the war are denounced as 'national traitors'. Many Russian-speaking Ukrainian writers have stopped writing in Russian, and some Russian poets have adopted the Ukrainian spelling of their names, but the Kopilka poets see themselves as defending the Russian language against the Putinites. As Anna Akhmatova wrote in 'Courage' (1942), 'we will preserve you, O great Russian speech'.

Meanwhile in Britain, Russian composers are blacklisted, Russian writers are removed from reading lists and the Stop the War movement is denounced as a tool of the Kremlin (twenty years ago, of course, it was the tool of Saddam Hussein). One of the consequences of the closing down of debate about the war has been the disappearance of Russian voices talking about the Russian experience of the conflict. The silencing of Russian voices outside Russia thus allows the Kremlin to claim that the whole of Russia supports the war.

Disbelief: 100 Russian Anti-War Poems, edited by Julia Nemirovskaya, was published by Smokestack on 1 January as a bilingual paperback and e-book. Translated by Maria Bloshteyn, Andrei Burago, Richard Coombes, Anna Krushelnitskaya and Dmitry Manin, the book includes poems by Polina Barskova, Vladimir Druk, Tatiana Volts-kaya, Mikhail Aizenberg and Tatiana Shcherbina.

At the time of writing the book has sold over 900 copies. While it has been ignored by the broadsheets and the BBC, Robert Chandler in the *Literary Review* has called it 'proof that the Russian language can still carry an antidote to the poisons disseminated by the Kremlin'. James Womack has described the book as an 'essential counterbalance to official news sources', that 'proves once again that in Russia poetry steps up when other voices fall silent'.

So far British poets have been notably quiet about this war. But then not many British poets have had much to say about any of the wars in the Falklands, Iraq, Yugoslavia, Afghanistan, Iraq (again), Libya, Yemen or Palestine.

Although the poets in *Disbelief* specifically address the war in Ukraine, this is a book about all stupid wars of this century – the civilian deaths, the refugees, the dishonest justifications, the media manipulations, the silences, the white noise and the absurd propaganda.

The poems in *Disbelief* are united by a common disbelief that anyone should try to resolve political disputes by war in the twenty-first century. And by a belief that poets must say this if no-one else will.

Are Philosophers Normal?

ZOHAR ATKINS

There is one view of philosophy that says it's not for everyone. The heroic temperament and mental acuity needed to question one's assumptions puts one at odds with mainstream society. The philosopher is a tragic figure, at least viewed from the outside, because he cannot integrate – like Socrates who asks annoying questions and then is made to drink the hemlock. The philosopher is threatening and abnormal viewed from without. Viewed from within, the philosopher is the only person not captive to conventional thinking, the only person with the courage to strive. Thus, the philosopher is equal parts outcast and self-aggrandizer (not unlike the Biblical Joseph, and not unlike many messianic figures). If you think of Marc Chagall's representation of the Jewish people as a kind of Jesus-like figure (or alternative to Jesus) you see the same chicken-or-egg pattern: are the Jews hated because they see themselves as a chosen people or are they a chosen people because they see themselves as chosen? Just as theological election and antisemitism are twinned, philosophical election and misosophy (hatred of wisdom) are twinned.

But the view of philosophy and philosophers as exceptional is not the only view, just as some Jewish thinkers have sought to tone down the theology of election, or, what amounts to the same thing, raise up many, if not all, peoples and traditions to the level of the elect. In America – a nation of immigrants – thinkers like Richard Rorty and Stanley Cavell sought to turn philosophy into something ordinary, something continuous with everyday life. Sartre and the French existentialists also sought to close the gap between philosophy and just hanging out in cafés. Sartre is said to have remarked that if you drink a glass of wine with awareness that can be a philosophical act, a kind of applied phenomenology. Walter Benjamin revived the idler, the teller of folktales, and the collector as quasi-philosophical characters. Heidegger and Wittgenstein, depending on how you read them, articulate a vision of philosophy as an attempt to unlearn conceptual attachment and cerebral idolatry and simply return to everyday life with new awareness. Wittgenstein says philosophy is more like therapy for philosophers who have gone astray than a view from the mountain-top. Before these movements, Nietzsche, in challenging the tradition from Plato to Hegel, made the case for style over substance: the excellent life is not the examined one, but the unique one, the creative one, the dynamic one.

In the old and standard view, philosophy is 'queen of the sciences'. In the more humble and typically more modern one, philosophy is a way of being in the world or an activity, not dissimilar to any other craft, be it writing verse, making films, cooking, or chatting about politics at the bar. There is something Zen-like in this second view of philosophy. But don't be fooled. The Zen masters still sat and sit for hours. Even if the goal is nothing extraordinary, it sure seems like a lot of effort is put into achieving that which cannot be achieved. Benjamin's idler is not lazy, nor is the Zen meditator complacent, nor is the Wittgensteinian philosopher passive. And so it is unclear if the second view of philosophy achieves the democratic and egalitarian sensibility that it poses at first blush. Ok, on the one hand, anyone can listen to John Cage, or compose 4'33 seconds of silence. But how many do? How many actually appreciate it? Perhaps even fewer than those who could follow Socrates's discourses. The egalitarian movement that treats philosophy as just one thing you could do, along with fly-fishing and juggling, may end up making a greater gadfly of philosophy than the one which aspired to create a class of philosopher-kings (or, according to Leo Strauss's recommendation, 'sects').

Here I am reminded of Rob Henderson's notion of 'luxury beliefs', a riff on Thorstein Veblen's idea of 'luxury goods'. People show off status not by purchasing flashy items, but by ascribing to views that they can afford to trumpet, even as the consequences are harmful or wasteful or simply absurd. Is the view that philosophy is a normal activity a luxury belief? Is the view that one is not chosen, and that all are equally special, not a kind of relativism that flattens the pathos of a calling?

I continue to toggle between the view that philosophy is extraordinary and the view that it is an activity like any other (just as the Israelites of the Book of Samuel sought to become a nation like all others.) But ironically, we must admit that nothing could be less normal than the aspiration to normalcy. Just as the German Jews sought to blend Jewishness and Germanness to the point of total assimilation, they were outed by German romantics and eventually turned into political enemies. Right as Hermann Cohen was saying that Judaism is a rational religion and the true expression of Kant, a storm was brewing. Do the ordinary philosophers not make a similar mistake? Perhaps they (we?) seek to assimilate too much to non-philosophy and should own their (our?) power more. Paradoxically, this may yield greater integration than a pseudo-hospitality which annuls the difference between philosophical life and normal life.

Letter from Wales

SAM ADAMS

I once tried reading Gwyn Thomas's 'Arrayed Like One of These' to a small, convivial audience. The narrator describes how he is taken by his father to the local drapers' shop in a south Wales mining valley to be measured for the suit of sub fusc then (and still) required for sitting Final Schools examinations at Oxford colleges. The father, blessed with a conviction that everyone needs and deserves a chance in life, insists that the young man who sweeps the shop floor should be handed the tape and take the measurements. The story goes on to describe how the misshapen garment that results so cramps and twists the wearer's posture in the examination hall that 'I wrote an essay on French writers in the modern period whose work was like a howl of pain from a trap of outrage and I could never have got the authenticity into the analysis if it had not been for the tailoring of Aaron Phipps'. As performance, my reading was a disaster: though familiar with the story, I was unable to control my own laughter as I read.

It is tempting to see a wild hint of allegory in the story. In 1931, from Rhondda County School for Boys, via School Certificate and Higher School Certificate, Thomas won a place at St Edmund Hall, Oxford, to study Spanish and French. Economically, the times were out of joint. Like most miners, his father was unemployed, and benevolent local institutions, also in straitened circumstances, reduced or stopped altogether grants to successful scholars. Unable to afford to dine in hall, he ate very badly: if it had not been for small sums provided by an older brother who was a teacher, he might have fared worse. He found himself in a student environment dominated by a moneyed class itself in political ferment, fans of Germany's national socialism pitted against those who favoured Russian communism. He was an outsider with only a few (though good) friends of similar background from other colleges, and an easy target. In February 1933, students of St Edmund Hall formally debated 'This House Prefers Germans to Welshmen'. Daryl Leeworthy, author of a new biography, *Fury of Past Time: A Life of Gwyn Thomas* (Parthian), is convinced this was a posh boys' waggish personal attack. The motion was carried with a large majority. Other than in intellectual capacity, the writer was as badly fitted for his Oxford college at that time as the suit of sub fusc that cramped the style of the character in his story.

Gwyn Thomas's father, Walter, the son of Welsh-speaking, post-Civil War immigrants to the USA, was born at Youngstown, Ohio, in 1873, though some time afterwards the family returned to Wales. He married Ziphorah (Davies) in 1893 and the couple set up home in Porth, a small town at the confluence of the Rhondda Fawr and Rhondda Fach, which owed its existence to coal, like all the other settlements up and down the valleys. Gwyn, born in 1913, was the last of their twelve children – not a remarkably numerous brood for the time, though the survival rate was impressive. Ziphorah died in 1919, aged forty-four, and an older sister, Hannah (Nan), became substitute mother to the youngest, who in his teens witnessed the strife of the coalfield in the 1920s and the depression of the 1930s, and then, as an essential part of his Oxford Spanish studies, spent the spring and summer of 1933 in Madrid, where the stirrings of political ferment that would explode into civil war in July 1936 were already apparent.

He left Oxford in debt to his college and began looking for work. Debilitated by a goitre and the operation for its removal, he abandoned his first teaching job in the Swansea valley within a day or so of starting and returned to Porth. There he eventually obtained irregular work tutoring WEA classes at the local Unemployed Club, only to discover that application of the Means Test meant that his earnings would be deducted from the dole dribbled out to his mineworker father. He left home and took a job at a Ministry of Labour Instructional Centre in Norfolk, teaching 'trainees' from the north-east of England, men (he wrote to his sister) 'of great strength, great dignity, who had their backs broken by an act of social idiocy'. Little wonder he described himself, again to Nan, as 'a communist ... profoundly committed to revolutionary principles'. Although later celebrated for his unique brand of humour, Thomas's political compass never veered from this leftward orientation.

Unfit for military service, he found modern language teaching posts in grammar schools, a couple of years in Cardigan and then in a move closer to home, Barry, a coastal town developed around docks constructed to export Rhondda coal. However much routine might have irked, the performative dimension of classroom teaching had an appeal, and he found time to write. He had published eleven novels and three collections of short stories, and begun to establish himself as a radio and television personality before he gave up teaching in 1962, tempted by a lucrative contract with the independent broadcaster TWW. In the later 1960s to '70s he turned playwright, with some successful West End runs. As a keen cinema-goer from childhood, he might even have achieved a celluloid apotheosis, initially via a stage production based on the life and personality of Aneurin Bevan in which Richard Burton was eager to play the leading role. Alas, the actor and film star could never quite find the time.

'Places like the Rhondda were parts of America that never managed to get on the boat' Thomas said. It is tempting to think his enjoyment of the movies and acknowledged regard for Damon Runyon, Chandler, Ring Lardner, Steinbeck, Hemingway and Wolfe were related to his father's Transatlantic origins, but the entire population of the Valleys was addicted to cinema and Runyonesque wise-guy gangster accents and tropes. These were widely imitated in the post-war years before the scope of everyday interests widened, and television entered every home. Nevertheless, one of the book's surprises is that the prose fiction of Gwyn Thomas was in all likelihood more widely read in the States than the poetry of his namesake Dylan, and gained a goodly share of favourable critical opinion.

Having made an exhaustive sweep of all available sources, Daryl Leeworthy concludes that he is the most significant Welsh writer of the twentieth century. The biography is manifestly accented by the author's political-historical viewpoint, which in this case appears entirely appropriate. Raymond Williams and Gwyn Alf Williams are recruited in support of the approach. The latter, whom I recall now as a magnetic personality and a firebrand among historians, is quoted as saying he regarded 'the corruption by poverty and depression of the great, crudely artistic, militant life of the Glamorgan valleys as one of the bitterest tragedies in the domestic history of Britain'. At one level Gwyn Thomas's writing is a celebration of the spirit of the Valleys' working class in countering the long years of hardship, and he brought an endlessly inventive wit to the task. Sharp social observation and satire underlie much of his writing, but it is often supremely amusing: the internet provides examples. Thomas was diabetic. Under the strain of broadcasting and related travel commitments his health deteriorated. He died in April 1981.

All Haulers

Conversation with Rimbaud's *Le Bateau ivre*

STAV POLEG

Comme je descendais des Fleuves impassibles,
Je ne me sentis plus guidé par les haleurs :
Des Peaux-Rouges criards les avaient pris pour cibles
Les ayant cloués nus aux poteaux de couleurs.

> It is always the water. The rain sets the evening in motion –
> the streetlamps throw light like metallic blue knives. All haulers
> are couriers of motion. If I'm guided by water
> let it be a river as furious as this.

J'étais insoucieux de tous les équipages,
Porteur de blés flamands ou de cotons anglais
Quand avec mes haleurs ont fini ces tapages,
Les Fleuves m'ont laissé descendre où je voulais.

> Indifference: to be free. The eye is a chamber, a field
> of blue lightnings. The harbour, an uproar of darkening
> stars. All haulers are couriers of water, all rivers
> are careless and flowing, forming new maps.

Dans les clapotements furieux des marées
Moi l'autre hiver plus sourd que les cerveaux d'enfants,
Je courus ! Et les Péninsules démarrées
N'ont pas subi tohu-bohus plus triomphants.

> Genesis 1. Some translations read *Tohu va-Vohu* as *without
> form.* Others as *void.* Others as both. Beginnings are messy. Choice
> is exhausting like the naming of water, each river
> and source. *And darkness was upon the face of the deep.*

La tempête a béni mes éveils maritimes.
Plus léger qu'un bouchon j'ai dansé sur les flots
Qu'on appelle rouleurs éternels de victimes,
Dix nuits, sans regretter l'œil niais des falots !

       Night vigils. There's a phone ringing in a far-off flat
       like a neon-blue flame, some music mixing nightfall with fireworks
       and light-sapphire rain. Somewhere a police car
       with a spiralling eye circles a lake.

Plus douce qu'aux enfants la chair des pommes sûres
L'eau verte pénétra ma coque de sapin
Et des taches de vins bleus et des vomissures
Me lava, dispersant gouvernail et grappin.

       Apples and childhood – it always works. The promise
       of knowledge, of urgent beginnings. Today I'm thinking
       of a sky raining blue wine as an exercise
       in hope. If you introduce an apple in the first act...

Et dès lors, je me suis baigné dans le Poème
De la Mer, infusé d'astres, et lactescent,
Dévorant les azurs verts ; où, flottaison blême
Et ravie, un noyé pensif parfois descend;

       To throw a stone like an incomplete thought
       into the darkening mirror of volatile stars. To dive
       and bring it back – I'm not sure how that works – water
       and depth, water and water –

Où, teignant tout à coup les bleuités, délires
Et rhythmes lents sous les rutilements du jour,
Plus fortes que l'alcool, plus vastes que nos lyres,
Fermentent les rousseurs amères de l'amour !

       Stronger than alcohol, louder than a night turning soundwaves
       and fire. All haulers are couriers of errors. Don't mistake
       water for depth. So much better to mistake it for love –
       a delirious flow under the bitter blossoming dark.

Je sais les cieux crevant en éclairs, et les trombes
Et les ressacs et les courants : je sais le soir,
L'Aube exaltée ainsi qu'un peuple de colombes,
Et j'ai vu quelquefois ce que l'homme a cru voir !

       I know winters: dawns exhausted by the promise
       of fire and snow. I know the city heavy with silver-pink
       fog, the lakes overfilling with ice and blue glass, the rain
       cutting through smoke. And I know the sunrise burning with dark.

J'ai vu le soleil bas, taché d'horreurs mystiques,
Illuminant de longs figements violets,
Pareils à des acteurs de drames très-antiques
Les flots roulant au loin leurs frissons de volets !

       From the ceiling, a yellow circle dips and settles, almost
       touching the ground. There's a lake made of metal-blue feathers,
       and a small paper boat in the ultra-violet light. In a film,
       a child draws and redraws the heart as a four-chambered map.

J'ai rêvé la nuit verte aux neiges éblouies
Baiser montant aux yeux des mers avec lenteurs,
La circulation des sèves inouïes,
Et l'éveil jaune et bleu des phosphores chanteurs !

On the stage, a model of a heart made of blue copper
and brass. The chambers are lanterns pulsing warm yellow
lights. It is snowing. The lake has vanished, the paper boat turned into
a map. A storm is approaching. All dreamers are carriers of night.

J'ai suivi, des mois pleins, pareille aux vacheries
Hystériques, la houle à l'assaut des récifs,
Sans songer que les pieds lumineux des Maries
Pussent forcer le mufle aux Océans poussifs !

Hysterical: for an entire blooming month. Coughing
blue algae and salt. The new-towering mountain was only
a castle made of whirlpool and coral-reef maps. Theatrical: for an entire
night. I'm drinking the full moon as a warm volatile heart.

J'ai heurté, savez-vous, d'incroyables Florides
Mêlant aux fleurs des yeux de panthères à peaux
D'hommes ! Des arcs-en-ciel tendus comme des brides
Sous l'horizon des mers, à de glauques troupeaux !

Flowers are distractions. Rainbows and panthers
are full-on distractions. Dreams, yes – interruptions. Gardens
and apples – how shall I put it? Everything
is a distraction. Childhood, childhood –

J'ai vu fermenter les marais énormes, nasses
Où pourrit dans les joncs tout un Léviathan !
Des écroulements d'eaux au milieu des bonaces
Et les lointains vers les gouffres cataractant !

In the beginning there was childhood. Chaos
was mistaken for choice. There was distance and more distance
but no doors. A river was turning into a map, a city
into a memory, a sea monster circling the ruins of a boat.

Glaciers, soleils d'argent, flots nacreux, cieux de braises!
Échouages hideux au fond des golfes bruns
Où les serpents géants dévorés des punaises
Choient, des arbres tordus, avec de noirs parfums!

On the stage, the boat is a metallic-blue spine, the lake is a relic –
the trace of a glacier. Take a picture of the silver suns, the ceiling
burning into orange embers. The dream devours
the seafloor, the garden, the serpent.

J'aurais voulu montrer aux enfants ces dorades
Du flot bleu, ces poissons d'or, ces poissons chantants.
– Des écumes de fleurs ont bercé mes dérades
Et d'ineffables vents m'ont ailé par instants.

Children, when they said the aquarium is open to the public
they meant closed. The beautiful blue is locked inside metal
and glass. The seahorse and sunfish are under construction. Let me
show you how to carry a storm in a box.

Parfois, martyr lassé des pôles et des zones,
La mer dont le sanglot faisait mon roulis doux
Montait vers moi ses fleurs d'ombre aux ventouses jaunes
Et je restais, ainsi qu'une femme à genoux...

    – almost there, part ocean part land: I'm an Other – a floating
    chamber, the woman on her knees holding onto the tenacity
    of shadow flowers, the vanity of water testing gravity and flight. All haulers
    are couriers of shadows. All chambers, carriers of sound –

Presque île, ballottant sur mes bords les querelles
Et les fientes d'oiseaux clabaudeurs aux yeux blonds
Et je voguais, lorsqu'à travers mes liens frêles
Des noyés descendaient dormir, à reculons !

    Those dark birds with yellow eyes – I have sent them away
    and named them *memories*. When they come back, they fly
    backwards to sleep – turning nights into castles of fire, chambers
    of blue-lightning fields, turning distance to maps.

Or moi, bateau perdu sous les cheveux des anses,
Jeté par l'ouragan dans l'éther sans oiseau
Moi dont les Monitors et les voiliers des Hanses
N'auraient pas repêché la carcasse ivre d'eau ;

    You are only sixteen and already you write: *I, a boat lost.*
    At sixteen I followed the boy carrying a canoe
    on his shoulders as if it were a light choice. The air
    was volatile and thickening with salt.

Libre, fumant, monté de brumes violettes,
Moi qui trouais le ciel rougeoyant comme un mur,
Qui porte, confiture exquise aux bons poètes,
Des lichens de soleil et des morves d'azur,

    – I'd vote for the smoke, the violet fog, the sky turning sand
    and red stone. All haulers are couriers of motion and I'm trying,
    I'm trying to hold onto the water, the river, the silver
    suns burning with snow –

Qui courais, taché de lunules électriques,
Planche folle, escorté des hippocampes noirs,
Quand les juillets faisaient crouler à coups de triques
Les cieux ultramarins aux ardents entonnoirs ;

    The stage is lit with electric-blue moons. Finally,
    the city. Finally, electricity. The sea is theatrical, the stars
    made of tempered-red glass. Summer is always too much. The sky
    bruised with ultramarine, the lakes heavy with light.

Moi qui tremblais, sentant geindre à cinquante lieues
Le rut des Béhémots et les Maelstroms épais,
Fileur éternel des immobilités bleues,
Je regrette l'Europe aux anciens parapets !

    In another country, the phone is still ringing, a car
    is still circling a lake like an unbroken thought, a dream feeding
    the night with a moon warm and burning, an island
    constructed out of more islands, more sunsets, more storms –

J'ai vu des archipels sidéraux ! et des îles
Dont les cieux délirants sont ouverts au vogueur :
– Est-ce en ces nuits sans fonds que tu dors et t'exiles,
Million d'oiseaux d'or, ô future Vigueur ?

> A constellation of archipelagos: phone calls, new cities, some
> letters, addresses, lost notes. Perhaps you wanted the water
> to carve out its own direction, offer new forms. All haulers
> are sea-wanderers, I get that, carriers of home.

Mais, vrai, j'ai trop pleuré ! Les Aubes sont navrantes.
Toute lune est atroce et tout soleil amer :
L'âcre amour m'a gonflé de torpeurs enivrantes
Ô que ma quille éclate ! Ô que j'aille à la mer !

> Moons are atrocious. I couldn't agree more. Suns
> are bitter, dark silver and cold. Love is acrid and swollen, light
> is intoxicating, apples are misleading, cities are made of warm
> misunderstandings, sunsets are false. Dawns are heartbreaking.

Si je désire une eau d'Europe, c'est la flache
Noire et froide où vers le crépuscule embaumé
Un enfant accroupi plein de tristesses, lâche
Un bateau frêle comme un papillon de mai.

> In the penultimate scene, a child sends a paper boat
> into the lake. Remember the apple? The moon was a distraction,
> the storm was a toss-up between memory and function, the garden
> was made of overrated sanctions – beautiful and cold.

Je ne puis plus, baigné de vos langueurs, ô lames,
Enlever leur sillage aux porteurs de cotons,
Ni traverser l'orgueil des drapeaux et des flammes,
Ni nager sous les yeux horribles des pontons.

> I'll go for the city's theatrical hybris, the traffic at night. All cities
> are couriers of motion. All lanterns, carriers of dusk. You will go on
> to write *Metropolitan,* trading rivers for new rivers and streets. All haulers
> are carriers of wonder. If I'm guided by water let it be this.

'Accent, Elaboration, Spontaneous Invention'

Whale Song and Subliminal Sound

LESLEY HARRISON

Our part of the coast was formed when Scotland lay south of the Equator. The climate was hot and very dry. A huge river flowed across the arid landscape leaving layers of sand and silt and gravel which, over millions of years, compacted to form a pebbly red sandstone. Over unimaginable time, the continent wheeled round and the river bed tilted out of the sea, cracking and sliding downhill, forming the buttresses and blowholes and tight inaccessible beaches that now edge the northern North Sea rim. The predominant background sound here is the soft roar of tons of multi-coloured egg stones being continually clawed and graded by the waves.

It was several months after I moved here that I realised the upturned boat mouldering away below was actually the carcass of a small whale. A humpback whale, in fact; an infant. A winter storm had left it on a ridge of sand and pebble at the foot of a steep, brambly slope. Depending on the tides, it sometimes sat proud of the beach on a pedestal of stones; at other times it was completely covered over.

Millions of years ago, a group of hoofed mammals left dry land and walked back into the water. Their tails turned into huge flukes; their legs disappeared into their sides; the apparatus between their mouth and ears dwindled. Now they move in an entirely different kinaesthetic environment, a world with its own depths and textures, its own time sequence, its own distances and tones.

The first thing a newborn whale hears is singing.

As a poet, the whole idea of making a poetry of or for a place, of inserting sound into that place, interests me greatly. There is an ethical, or poethical, dimension to this which becomes more acute as the scale and depth of the environmental degradation we have perpetrated becomes apparent. Language is the process by which we create ourselves, grammatically and referentially, as the figure-in-the-landscape. 'Language is dependent on relationships and as such immediately inscribes ethical terms', says John Wrighton. Its central terms are the verb 'to be' and the pronoun 'I', and in using these we gather the world around ourselves. Language is so deeply inhabited, so intrinsically self-orientated, that it reveals a phenomenological prioritisation of the self as soon as we speak.

There is also a practical, technical dimension. 'I don't write for my tongue, but I do write for my ear', says Fiona Sampson. 'I imagine the poem being spoken out loud and not by me, in other words I imagine a series of sounds in silence: I imagine the poem being *sounded out*.' I am, however, not sure if it is possible to make a categorical distinction between hearing and speaking: as language users, and as poets especially, we play with the texture of language, with the shape and lie of sounds in the mouth, with 'language lined with flesh... the whole presence of the human muzzle' (Barthes). Language is both embodied and performative. It is also site-specific, relying on the 'flashes, ruptures and sudden displacements' (Kristeva) of denotation and grammatical rule which we abide by and then transgress, with a wink to our audience. We 'play' with pattern and repetition, metaphor and metonymy, rhythm and timbre, to generate and renew meaning within our social group. Now, 'languaging' is a collusive act, and a process which presumes prior occupation of a common ground.

I wonder also if we can imagine language as a 'series of sounds in silence'. Does our sonic landscape – wind, trees, rooms, traffic – reflect back in the qualities and adjustments of our own voice? What do we hear, even at a subliminal level, that affects how we shape our own word sounds? This is a question that I imagine is impossible to answer. It does, however, make me think about the rich, fluid landscape of sound in which we are always immersed, which enters through our pores and permeates all our thinking. 'Hugh MacDiarmid used to speak about the human brain being largely unused', said Edwin Morgan when discussing the multilingualism and sound experimentation in his own poetry. 'I'm sure that's quite true, and I think language is like that too'. It also makes me think of all that we have become dulled to, or have lost, the volume of which is immeasurable.

For us humans, most sound is detected through the eardrums and transmitted to the cochlea or inner ear. In some cases, however, vibrations are conducted through the body and picked up directly by the inner ear, as when you stick your fingers in your ears and sing. With practice, the listener can detect fine differences of pitch, texture, rhythm and dynamics. 'My awareness of the acoustics in a concert venue is excellent', says percussionist Evelyn Glennie. 'For instance, I will sometimes describe an acoustic in terms of how thick the air feels.' With very low frequency vibration, the human ear starts becoming inefficient and the rest of the body's sense of touch starts to take over. Composer Oliver Beer has created pieces using the natural resonances of buildings and spaces – pieces which cannot be recorded, but must be experienced in that time and place.

In composition, there is a musical distinction between the simple absence of planned sound – what acousticians call 'white noise' – and a rich 'held silence'. This is the moment where the conductor raises the baton and all fall silent in anticipation. This silence is already part of the composition, as are all the other metered breaks or intuitive pauses between phrases, played, sung or spoken; as is the white space around and within the poem on the page.

As with language, music has both a performative and a transactional aspect. The singer or composer 'plays' with the audiences' expectations, with deviations from rehearsed, grammatical patterns, using emphasis, hiatus and other articulatory effects as well as spontaneous invention. These experiments with transgression are key: they presuppose a knowing audience, and reveal the singer's self-positioning within this wider community of singers, and within the mesh of iterations of this song.

Whale sound remains mysterious. The ear canals for both toothed and baleen whales are vestigial and no longer connected to the ear drum, and both pitch and volume are thought to be detected entirely through bone conduction. Depending on the species, their songs may fall partially within the range of human hearing. Toothed whales emit high-pitched, ultra-sonic clicks to echolocate prey and perceive their environment in fine resolution. By contrast, baleen whales can vocalize and hear very low-pitched sound, which can travel great distances and scatter to large areas in water. Fin whale pulses are short 'down' sweeps that extend well below human hearing and can be detected over 3,000 miles away. The song of the blue whale is alleged to be comparable with experiencing an earth tremor. Using low frequency sound, along with layers of salinity and warm/cool water in the ocean, baleen whales can moan or sing for each other over areas as large as an ocean basin. Dissection of their throats reveals what are still recognisably vocal cords now tucked away in fleshy sacs that line the larynx. It is thought that, while underwater, they can move air between these sacs and their lungs, generating long infrasonic melodies without losing air.

Interestingly, in my readings of eighteenth- and nineteenth-century whaling journals, so far I have found only one reference to whalers actually hearing whales sing, and this story too is second hand. Herbert Lincoln Aldrich, a newspaper journalist, travelled with the New Bedford Whaling Fleet in 1887, and afterwards wrote a travel book and a series of popular articles about his experiences. Aldrich recounts a story which he first thought to be another tall tale, but later realised was widely believed. Some seasons previously, several ships were moored side-by-side waiting for the ice to shift, the captains 'gamming' together on deck, when one suddenly interrupted with a shout: 'There's a bowhead!' Despite initial ridicule, the outcome was the capture of several whales and a new respect for any whaler who was believed to be able to hear whales as they swam below. Aldrich describes the vocal sounds they made, including when struck by harpoons: 'with bowhead-whales the cry is something like the hoo-oo-oo of the hoot-owl, although longer drawn out, and more of a humming sound than a hoot. Beginning on F, the tone may rise to G, A, B, and sometimes to C, before slanting back to F again. With the humpbacked-whale, the tone is much finer, often sounding like the E string of a violin.' He also notes 'singing is almost never heard in the Arctic', which was probably true. To pick up this song on the deck of a ship would require incredibly still conditions. Also, the most accessible whale songs to our ears are those of the humpback, which sings mostly during the mating season in May/June in warmer waters.

Sound travels much better through water than through air, and the hull of a ship may act like a huge shell in which all sea sounds are amplified. However, even below deck, the right conditions for listening would hardly ever occur. In the internet chat room of the Nautical Research Guild, the question 'What does it sound like to be inside an XVIII century whaling ship?' generated a consensus around this point. 'A wooden ship at sea is an orchestration of wood working against wood. A lot of groaning and creaking and this is increased with the increase in sea state... The larger ships would have a deeper sound... you can hear the water below deck, through the hull. Below the waterline you can hear sounds as well. I heard whales once.' And an ex-submariner describes the whole-body impact of the sonar of a ship passing overhead – 'it was irritating beyond belief' – and of a helicopter: 'the noise of the Helo transmitted through the water, down to our submarine, through the hull and into our ears'.

On this stretch of coast, the waves raking stones on the beach generates a grey sound that (most days) is indistinguishable from the wind that fills your head, and which I imagine as textured like felt, carrying an audible friction from where it has dragged across stubble fields, or hedges, or the scree slopes behind. I often wonder if we actually hear rain coming: there is certainly a sensation, a wave of cold air ahead of it. A few years back a whole section of scrubby woods nearby was cleared to make another cereal field, and I was sure I could hear a gap where something was missing – some strand of earth sound, some kind of altered air.

There are obvious reasons why we empathise with the plight of the whale above other species, and why they offer an easy barometer to the health of our seas, and our own porous, fraying habitat. Their size is irrefutable; there is the imaginative and emotional impact of their death. The Cuvier's beaked whale inhabits waters below 1,000 feet and has the deepest and longest recorded dives of any whale species. Despite this, it is one of the most frequently beached cetaceans. In 2018, in the space of weeks, 118 were washed up on the coasts of Ireland, the Hebrides, Iceland and the Faroes – the largest global stranding in the world, and just a fraction, no doubt, of the actual mortality rate. All were already dead and many in an advanced state of decomposition, indicating a catastrophic event out at sea but making post-mortem examination difficult. The cause is now accepted to have been mid-frequency active sonar – sound which doesn't die away in moments, but exists for months, pulsing across vast oceanic distances. Its source was Joint Warrior, the largest NATO exercise in Europe, which operated that year out of Faslane on the Clyde. (For more information, see Mhairi Killin's project 'On Sonorous Seas'). A very quick Google search reveals lists of other multiple strandings associated with military or mining or drilling activity. The impact on other marine species which use echo-location – krill, all forms of fish, seals and walrus, diving birds? – is less visible, and so difficult to form a proactive response around.

Whales have a semi-mythical place in our culture. 'For what would an ocean be without a monster lurking in the dark?' asks Werner Herzog. 'It would be like sleep without dreams.' They generate awe, and humility.

Humpbacks play for three times longer than they hunt, creating huge extended games that range right across the ocean. They subtly alter the shape of their bodies to slip between thermoclines and layers of current, gliding a mile down, dropping their heart beat, collapsing their lungs to adjust to the pressure. They use the rotation of the planet, magnetic and lunar currents and the contours of the seabed to find their way south to mate. Once the calf is born, it needs to be exposed to the air before its blow hole opens and it begins to breathe. Its mother nudges it to the surface, and helps it learn to swim.

Composer and zoömusicologist Alex South has been exploring the music-like aspects of humpback calls, both for creative purposes and to see how far the human–cetacean coincidence can be argued. Zoömusicology raises the question of whether the use of sound communication among animals has an aesthetic component; it asks whether the whale's 'song' goes beyond what is needed simply for communication. This begs Kristeva's question, of course, of whether meaning is also generated in affective, playful transgression in collusion with its audience. Whales also have a very well-developed capacity for imitation.

Humpback singers can be heard great distances away, though usually singers are on average five kilometres apart. Where they are numerous, several songs can go on at once – 'an a-synchronous chorus' – with no attempt (it seems) to co-ordinate. Humpback songs usually evolve over time by a slow lengthening and the addition of new pulses, so that after five to ten years the original song is unrecognisable. Only the male sings, hanging head down in the water, usually at night, and for up to twenty-two hours. Whale biologists define a song as ten to thirty minutes of sustained singing, though are noncommittal regarding whether the beginning and end points are behavioural or acoustic. A song unit usually lasts a few seconds, followed by an equal period of silence.

Alex experiments with recordings to try to isolate these units – the shortest block of repeated sounds that are distinguishable to the human ear – and their patterns of repetition, or enhancements, or improvisations. These become more audible when recordings are speeded up, which makes clearer (to our ears) the hierarchical structure of phrases, pitch steps and melodic intervals. However, Alex points out, even when the human listener has isolated these phrases and created refined, sometimes notated descriptions of them, there is no guarantee that the whale also thinks in terms of these structures and patterns, or is singing in a time frame that we can grasp.

For me, one consequence of this comparison of our language-in-place and that of another species is that we must re-evaluate the relationship between human sound-making and the environment in which it is made. It becomes difficult now to think of our experience of music, or language, or any sound gesture as separate from the place in which and for which it was created and in which it is heard, with all its ambient and incidental noise. Adding sound gesture to the world presupposes and imagines how it will be heard across the distance it must travel, and who will hear it at the other side.

More importantly, the gaps in our knowledge are abyssal: the soundscape in which we now live is radically altered, and radically impoverished, both within our range of hearing and beyond its borders; and we have no way of knowing how more subtle, subliminal sounds affect our sense of location and belonging, and how their absence is leaving us stranded. How would we know?

NOTES

Oliver Beer – www.oliverbeer.co.uk
Mhairi Killin – www.onsonorousseas.com
Alex South – soundcloud.com/alex-south-music

Three Poems

MAUREEN MCLANE

Solstice (Brunswick Square Gardens)

In this tree light congeals
into leaves more deeply serrated
by time and crossbreeding
than those of the kindred plane nearby –
rhododendron's invasive, a sycamore's
a kind of maple. Knowing that,
what do I know. That I talked
with you yesterday and trust you –
that I learn by ear a social ear –

'Nothing in a garden is forever.
That's why you've got to love it.'

Let's jump the asymptotic limit
of infinite green and shining
anonymous orgasms.

The day suspended between an almost gone spring
and a summer unlaunched.

You wear the clouds as if you were accustomed to an open sky.

Deflection: an Ode

*– lines mainly composed
some four miles south of & then at
Raquette Lake, NY*

for Anahid Nersessian

That gray light
that lingers in the west
portends what   something | something
Ana that might not arrive
directly, or ever. What is certain
to come is night by the light
of reading Hegel as if I were Marx
right now and he i.e. Hegel were saying Now
Is Night. In translation. Now here it's dusk
and the owl and the deer at the Great Camp
were unbothered when I drove up
looking for human trails.
        Another dumb human.
The wind nor howls
nor moans it's just barely there
so let's call it air caressing
the ice-crystalling snow mounded and heaped
along roadsides, in the woods and on branches –
the cedars' long drooping arms.

When is a heap of snow
or sand no longer a heap?
Must we sow that we reap?
What did the solitary reaper reap
but a song and some grain | the grain massed
in a heap the song become an alien air
in someone else's poem.

Alone alone all all
alone on a snowy mountain
a sudden thought of bobcats
and bears gave fright: a timely
utterance gave that thought
relief and a testing
of my emergency whistle
which better far
until calamity
were mute.

O Ana!
We receive but what we give.
No. There is no law
karmic or golden
of reciprocity or equilibrium
even Newton's broken
along a quantum wave and the thing
Arendt said would utterly transform
the human condition as we know it
 – 'an emigration of men from the earth
to some other planet' – has almost happened
or has eons since in the multiverse.

It's all in the almost, most
of it, the unlived lives which are our lives
despite. Should I be talking
about something serious like fashion
& not the overdetermined weather?
Are you sick 'of it all'?
        Is it the loophole
of retreat one seeks
or total immersion in the given a flow
a self-forgetfulness like a seal
in water one imagines,
fatally, anthropomorphic.

There I go –
no way around it –
imagining other
minds and now your child
grown toddler steps boldly,
lightly, now onto a glass table, now on grass,
into the given transformable world.

Actual dusk.
I step out on this lake.
Two winters, with the length
of two long winters. It takes no courage
so to step the very snowmobilers
brave it | Raquette Lake

become a frozen gliding surface
for their motored skis. But always
a stepping westward onto a lake
belies the memory
of summer, wild sun, blue-gray water
lapping the shore, the boaters
and sailors inadvertent geometers
of the space this water's made.

A hundred years ago
they harvested this lake
for ice | the ice cut hauled stored
under hay in sheds then cubed
into the swankest drinks
we'll never quite drink, cocktails
from the '20s, since the 1920s
are gone though the 2020s are upon us
& in the mind of an almost dead god
(by which I might mean Fredric Jameson
or Coleridge pantheist and certain Buddhists
and string theorists) all times and places
perforce co-exist.

We shall go walking
with Laura some day in the Lake District, say
in five years, and we can see
what they saw Dorothy and William
and sad ecstatic Coleridge and clever
De Quincey deranging himself.
        We could bring a friend
to the Goody Blake Restaurant
in Grasmere and get pedestrian
and theoretical with Celeste. You could write
long letters to Hazlitt and we could text
Byron and some living poets you admire.
Surely there is some leftover opium
to smoke in Dove Cottage. The lakes
and tarns and slopes outlast thus far
any lines of verse or prose. We could steal
a rowboat or pay the Roma proprietor
to take one of his boats out on the lake.

You could say this
is a utopia, however
or precisely because
        limited.

I have been long
about this business
if the darkening sky
is our measure. Is it?
The world's a hologram
of itself some say
not me. Colors resolve
into ever fewer, the angle
of sun deflecting
their hues toward a gray scale
our cats can see right through.

This has not been Earl's Beer
and Cheese, this bar, the Tap Room
of Raquette Lake, when on a day
early in the New Year
I sat (unlike Wordsworth
with his water) with a beer
and collected long thoughts I've had
toward you, Ana,
as the Adirondack day moves downward
to darkness and the midafternoon sun
of LA surely shines imperturbable as an Aeolian lute
untroubled by any wind.

Sunflowers

This is the time of sunflowers who tell time
in fields poems stone and to the willing eye falling
on their stupendous composite flanged faces bursting
from burdened stems jammed in ceramic urns or thrusting
up from an earth precisely planted for mechanical harvest

This is the time of missing bodies missing
in their own lives and bodies gone
missing the painting bringing the orifice back
to its plugged and rimmed edges. This is the time of repatriation
rendition unrendered. Nothing extraordinary

in the life of Dorothy Wordsworth except her mind
and passionate walking. Crushed shells make a cliff
and women the unread and what some call unlived.
Someone fell into a black painting a black hole
they discovered was real both black and a hole

and they fell and they fell but escaped all black holes
are not blackholes and the dark face of the sunflower

Six Poems

FABIO MORÁBITO

Translated by Richard Gwyn

1. To Get to Puebla

So many years without knowing how to get to Puebla,
which junction of which artery you have to take
to get to Puebla,
only two hours distant!
People go to Puebla and return
the same day,
I myself have been to Puebla
(who hasn't been to Puebla?)
and so many years without knowing how to get there!

Show me how to get to Puebla,
which is two hours distant,
and to believe in God,
who is so close that He can be reached
and returned from the same day.
I myself have believed in God
(who hasn't believed in God?)
The same thing happens with Him as with Puebla,
I don't know which junction of which artery to take.

What has become of my life
that I haven't learned what everyone knows:
to speak with God and to visit and return from Puebla the same day?
I only know the road to Cuernavaca,
that's the only way I know to leave this city.

Show me the road to Puebla,
show me how to leave, to believe, to go
and return the same day.

2. *In Limine*

By the mercy of the sea
all beaches are born
for no reason and in no order,
one every thousand years,
one every hundred seas.

I was born on a beach
in Africa, my parents
took me north
to a hectic city,
today I live in the mountains.

I got used to the altitude
and I don't write in my language,
on certain days of the year
I suffer from fainting fits and vertigo,
the plain returns to me,

I leave for whatever sea I can,
I take books that I don't read,
that I never even opened,
the birds write
more subtle stories.

My sea is this sea,
defenseless, at first light,
it yields to the earth weapons,
toys, bunches
of algae, its whims,

it migrates like a circus,
leaves everything fallow:
the sea's debris
that women love
like an older sister.

For the one who turns his back
on everything, I come
face to face with it all;
for the one who loses his edge,
I gain origins, land,

I gasp my varied and
solitary alphabet
and finally find my nomadic
desert tongue,
my true land.

3. Invisible Dog

I have an invisible dog,
I carry a quadruped inside me
that I let out in the park
just as others do with their dogs.
When I bend down
to let him go free,
to play and run,
the other dogs chase him,
only their owners don't see him,
maybe they don't see me either.
It happens more and more with every outing
the other dogs get worked up into a state
and among the owners a disquiet grows
and they call their dogs
to prevent a pack from forming.
Maybe they don't see me either,
sitting on a bench,
doubled over a little
with the effort of letting him go free,
and although they can't see him,
perhaps they do see the dog
they carry inside,
invisible like my own,
the beast they never release,
the dog that they repress
while taking their dogs for a walk.

4. Farewell

On Tuesdays
a beggar used to come
with a mandolin
to the shade of the citron tree
beneath our window
with its green shutters
that my mother would open
to give him two apples;
one day we moved,
went far away,
on Tuesday the beggar came
to our abandoned house
and I know he was there
a long time playing
his mandolin
beneath our window
in the shade of the citron tree
before leaving for ever
the hill
where our house stood.

5. As Before a Meadow

As before a meadow a cow
placidly lowers her head
and only raises it to count her blessings,
or like a whale parked directly
in the path of migrating plankton,
sometimes I surprise myself, stalled
and overwhelmed, parked
amid the great meadow of language.
But I don't have two stomachs
and even the cow seeks out, samples, chooses,
singles out a special grass that pleases her,
the meadow is not an Eden, it's her job,
and the whale, when he eats plankton,
filters out the coarser elements,
winning his daily bread, his immense bread,
seeking it out in the deeps of the sea,
later emerging to expel the devil from his body
and returning beneath the waves without knowing
whether he is eating plankton or breathing it.
It's not easy being a cetacean or a ruminant
and I don't have a double stomach, and even with one

I have to choose, not everything is suitable,
only poetry doesn't cast aside,
regards the world before eating.
Fasting world, how do you taste?
To be able to consume one single meal that lasts a
     lifetime,
that with a single meal we are sated
and have a lifetime to digest it...
to have an immense capacity for assimilation
to know that everything's digested
and what is lost makes a detour and returns.
This is why I write: to recover
from the depths all that adheres there,
because it is the only detour in which I believe,
because to write opens a second stomach
in the species.
Verse with its acid removes the particles
left behind by the plankton of days
and from me also, like the cetacean,
a jet of water springs forth from time to time,
a vertical word that breaks the tedium of the seas.

6. Sobbing

I always arrive late
at funerals,
when the eyes
of those attending
have dried
and some have already forgotten
the face of the deceased,
how old he was,
the cause of his death.
Then I arrive
with my anachronistic weeping,
in my honest mourner's black
and like a conflagration
I offer out hugs,
clasp the hands of the widow
and of the orphans
between my hands,
the whole cortège witnesses
my pain,
no one dares refute it,
people are embarrassed
and crowd together again
around the dead man,
the widow caves in
and breaks into sobs,
the orphans also
and the sound of weeping grows once more,

reaching everyone,
those who have not yet wept,
those who are there
who observe that it is the weeping
of a returning tide
of considerable magnitude,
and they enter into it,
they forget about their dead
or remember them with greater clarity,
and the weeping flows faster,
dragging with it the weeping of other occasions,
its roar warns of a great weeping
which broadens out
and detaches itself from the dead,
for this I arrive late
at the weeping of others,
I come with another weeping
in my throat
which I let loose among the damp bodies
and I see how it clings to every tear
coils around,
crackles in each of them,
and I am the only one who knows
it is my misfortune
they are weeping for,
that they are weeping for my dead
and bestow their weeping on me.

From the Archive

from *PNR* 170, Volume 32 Number 6, 2006

Birdwatching Poem

In the twigs, *contorta*, of two trees
which the council has planted by the new
apartment block - eight waxwing, bibbed, masked and
crested. At first they were conclusive black
up there in silhouette, then they flourished
down in splendid grey and cinnamon, dashed
out with writs of zinc and red. The tails tipped
in gold. A hundred years ago, Mützel
engraved them, posed in conifers and birch. [...]

R.F. LANGLEY

more available at www.pnreview.co.uk

from *What Is Poetry?*

PHILIP TERRY

Less studied, more spontaneous, much rawer, unrhymed, Auden's marginalia are among his greatest poems:

> Small tyrants, threatened by big,
> sincerely believe
> they love Liberty.
> ...
>
> A dead man
> who never caused others to die
> seldom rates a statue.

To spend a lifetime in poetry, only to find that what you almost threw away was your best work.

*

The editors transcribe this as follows: 'was never / Frigate li / like'. Where the editors see 'li' at the end of the second line, anticipating the word 'like' in the subsequent line, I see the letter 'w', taking us back to the 'w' that begins the poem, if we can call it a poem, in the word 'was'. And this changes how I read the poem. 'W' here stands for woman – something that Dickinson underlines by writing this particular 'w' (not all Dickinson's w's look like this, frequently they are more angular, smaller, spikier) so as to accentuate its resemblance to the human breasts. So the fragment reads: 'was never / Frigate w(oman) / like'. Which makes an immediate kind of sense: Frigates are never like women *or* Frigates are never womanly. A frigate, up until the mid-twentieth century, referred to a war-vessel, capable of carrying up to sixty guns, sometimes more. This was *no place for women*, and conditions on these ships were harsh. Some-

times they would be at sea for upwards of a year. Until the introduction of steam ships, they were powered by sails, the foremost of which was triangular in shape, like the flap of the envelope on which Dickinson writes these lines, and which hung just above where the figurehead of the ship would normally be. Yet the first American frigates, built in the 1790s, such as the USS *Constitution*, which Emily Dickinson may well have seen moored in Boston harbour, did not have figureheads, which were considered idolatrous by the naval designers of the time. The figureheads had been taken away, just as decorations in churches had been torn down in the Reformation, and just as the envelope on which Dickinson writes has been torn, and just as the word w(oman) in the poem has been torn, reduced to a single letter, 'w'. If, on the simplest level, 'frigates' are not like 'women' because 'women' are not warlike, are not powerful, are not given to achieving their ends through violence, Dickinson here opens these meanings up further to hint at other senses related to the warlike nature of the frigate, suggesting that the war here goes further than the protection of the American shores, frequently from British ships, but expands to include the war of the sexes, the erasure of women from history, and, like Dickinson in her lifetime, from literary history. Yet if, on one level, the torn envelope encodes all this in its message – the erasure of women – on another level, it says the opposite – it cries out in protest, the removed letters of the word 'woman', 'oman', metamorphosing into the cry 'Oh, man!' – the torn sail enacts a castration of the vessel, a disabling of the vessel of war and of male power. And if you tilt the image backwards by 60° it comes to resemble a cartoon caricature of a man – now the 'w' comes to represent his eye, and perhaps suggests 'man' seen through the eyes of 'women', or even *what* 'man' sees when he looks at 'woman' – a man in a wig, perhaps, with a penis (or a pen?) for a nose, a man who bears more than a passing resemblance to Thomas Jefferson, author of the Declaration of Independence, whose idea of universal suffrage had extended to all males, but not to slaves nor to women. Like.

*

Keats's letter of 15 May 1817 to his brothers George and Tom, where he discusses 'negative capability', and Rimbaud's of 13 May 1871 to Georges Izambard where he declares 'I is another' (a phrase, when put into English, which is curiously encrypted in the recipient's name, '*I's am bard*'), not only have symmetries in their dates and addressees, but in their arguments: for both writers poetry involves a forgetting of the self, a 'going out'. This is echoed by a much later letter, published in Jack Spicer's chapbook of 1957, *Admonitions*, where he writes: 'The trick naturally is what Duncan learned years ago and tried to teach us – not to search for the perfect poem but to let your way of writing of the moment go along its own paths, explore and retreat but never be fully realized (confined) within the boundaries of the poem.' Spicer, here, brings the insights of Keats and Rimbaud down to the very materiality of the poem at the moment of its coming into being. His remarks on his own early poems, which he regards as failures, are illuminating: 'They are one night stands filled (the best of them) with their own emotions, but pointing nowhere, as meaningless as sex in a Turkish bath. It was not my anger or frustration that got in the way of my poetry but the fact that I viewed each anger and each frustration as unique – something to be converted into poetry as one would exchange foreign money.' This commodification – confining of emotion, of the poet, and of poetry itself – the hallmark of capitalism, is the precise opposite of the 'going out', the disappearance of self, the venture-that-is-the-poem that is gestured towards in these three great letters.

*

Around 1950, the invention of the Photofit Picture or Identikit, used by the police and the judiciary, relied on the principle of the combination of diverse elements used to reconstitute the broad outline of a suspect's face. The same principle of combination has played a role in the history of art and literature, stretching back to the combinatorial poems of Raymond Queneau, whose *A Hundred Thousand Billion Poems* (1961) is composed of cut horizontal strips, giving a vertiginous multiplicity of possible readings when one chooses lines of the poem from across the book, to the portraits of Giuseppe Arcimboldo in the sixteenth century, made entirely of fruits, vegetables, flowers, fish and books. The French for 'Identikit', 'Portrait-Robot', supplies the title for a collection of fifty poem-portraits by the minimalist poet Michèle Métail, first published in 1982 in the Bibliothèque Oulipienne n° 21, subtitled 'Mental imagery in the manner of Arcimboldo and Nicolas de Larmessin'. Here, Métail makes her portraits out of selections of ready-made language – perhaps with a nod to Marcel Duchamp's readymades – clichés and fixed phrases repeated without a thought, and reproduced in dictionaries as in speech: the arm of a chair, the foot of a mountain, the mouth of a river, the eye of a needle. Such phrases, by virtue of their polysemy, as soon as one plays with their literal and figurative meanings, suggest metamorphosis, and in so doing take us back to the art of Arcimboldo, and to the composite figures found in paleolithic caves, a man with a wrack of antlers on his head, a figure with the head of a bird. Here's one of Métail's poem-portraits, from a more recent collection, translated into English as 'Identikits':

THE MUSEUM CURATOR

LARGE FRAME
HEAD OF A NAIL
EYE OF THE MASTER
ARTISTIC SENSE
MEMBERS OF THE ACADEMY OF FINE ARTS
BRONZE BUST

HEIGHT OF FAME
FOOT OF A LAMP
EXPERIMENTAL TITLE
PICTURE PERFECT

If, ordinarily, we think of poetry as being the opposite of cliché – the one thing the poem cannot tell us is that the sky is blue – here Métail paradoxically makes poetry *out of* clichés, but in so doing *unhinges* the cliché, peels it back, at once deconstructing and reconstructing it in a single move, akin to magic, which releases the power of language we thought the cliché had extinguished.

*

Idea for a conceptual poem: the text of Eliot's *The Waste Land* displayed digitally (as part of an exhibition for its centenary). Each day, for the duration of the exhibition, a word is removed. By the close of the exhibition, nothing remains of Eliot's text but blank space.

*

'Poetry consists in general of the arrangement of an arbitrary – fictive – *form* with an arbitrary – fictive – sense.' (Paul Valéry). *Discuss.*

*

My dear Monsieur d'Orfer
It's like getting punched, when, for an instant, all you see is stars! your brusque injunction –
'Define Poetry'
I stammer, murdered:
'Poetry is the expression, in human language, returned to its essential rhythm, of the mysterious sides of certain aspects of existence: in this it bestows authenticity on our stay and constitutes the only trace of spirituality.'
Goodbye; and send my apologies.
STÉPHANE MALLARMÉ

*

Poetry, Texas. The Danish poet Pejk Malinovski came across the town of Poetry, Texas, on Google. There was a spherical water tower, resembling a giant ear syringe, with the word Poetry on it. 'The temptation to go to Poetry', he says, 'was too great. It's real and it's a metaphor.' He documented his visit for radio in 2012. It is a magical piece, at once a meditation on the ordinary and the extraordinary, where even the most mundane thing, because it takes place, or exists, in Poetry, a gas pump, a fence, a ditch, a disused quarry, is transformed into metaphor. His GPS brings him to the gas station, the *centre* of Poetry, which he makes his base. 'What is Poetry?' he asks the people he meets. 'What I call Poetry, and what other people call Poetry, is about four different things', says the Mayor of Poetry. 'Poetry is expanding', he adds, 'everyone wants to live in Poetry.' Another interlocutor says: 'People want to know what hard work is, come and spend a day in Poetry.' Robert Weed, the Pastor of Poetry, takes him round some of the houses at the *edge* of Poetry, surrounded by fences. They arrive at a dry creek, The Bottoms, that marks the border of Poetry. 'Once you get on the other side of Poetry,' says the Pastor, 'there's just nothing there.' If, for Robert Frost, poetry is what is *lost* in translation, in Poetry, Texas, everything that is *found* becomes poetry. 'What is Poetry?' Malinovski wonders again, before leaving, for there is nowhere to sleep in Poetry. 'Maybe it's a way of being in the world?'

*

'What is Poetry', a poem by John Ashbery, in his 1975 collection *Houseboat Days*, has a title that looks like a question, but it doesn't have a question mark. So perhaps Ashbery intends us to read it as a statement: not 'What is Poetry?', but *'What* is Poetry', in other words poetry is defined by its whatness, its thingness, which reminds me of William Carlos Williams's statement 'No ideas but in things'. Which is borne out by the following, from lines five and six of the poem: 'Trying to avoid // Ideas, as in this poem?' Yet, to complicate things, Ashbery, here as elsewhere in the poem, does now use a question mark, as if he were answering an initial question, 'What is Poetry?', which invites the reader to read the statement of the title *also* as a question, inserting the missing question mark herself. And perhaps this present / absent question mark itself plays a role in defining the poem, poetry – like Wittgenstein's duck/rabbit, it takes on a different aspect depending on how we look at it. It is unsettled, and unsettling. And Ashbery doesn't stop here: his poem gives us other, alternative answers, to the trace of a question, all of which can, in one way or another, stand in for potential definitions of poetry: 'Beautiful images?', 'The snow // That came when we wanted it to snow?' The snow is an image, a thing, but it also contains an idea: snow may be beautiful, but it melts, and in its melting it brings thoughts of disappearance, decay, death, as in Villon's line: 'But where are all the snows of yesteryear?' (untranslatable, according to Stephen Rodefer, but that's another matter). And this in turn reminds us that poems, even when they have *no ideas but in things*, also contain ideas; they mostly can't help it. Even if the ideas run through the poem like an underground stream, working by gesture rather than direct statement, as opposed to the poetry of ideas, of which instagram poetry is a recent manifestation. It's bad imagism, in other words, as we might be taught in school, which is bereft of ideas. Something which Ashbery gestures towards in the lines: 'In school / All the thought was combed out…' And perhaps Ashbery's poem is there to remind us of this, that even when poetry has no ideas but in things, it shouldn't be forgotten that these things are the richer when they embody, however ambiguously, ideas. Good imagism doesn't just give us an image, a thing, it makes us think, too. And as it does so, the statement becomes a question, the missing question mark returns, like the return of the repressed, as in the final line of Ashbery's poem, where the 'what?' reappears, this time with a question mark.

*

The Penguin Book of the Prose Poem, edited by Jeremy Noel-Tod, is a beautiful collection. It contains an eclectic gathering of many gems, from Baudelaire and Mallarmé, to Anne Carson and Jeff Hilson, and the first time I read it, I immediately picked it up and read it again. I would happily read it again now. There is one type of prose poem, though, that it does not feature, and that does not feature in any discussions of prose poetry that I know of, and that is the poem that *looks* like a poem – it has lines that don't go all the way to the right-hand margin – but *reads* like prose. Ron Padgett's poems are often of this kind. His poem 'Method', from his collection *How to Be Perfect* (2007), is as good an example of this as I can find:

> Who else would you like to know about?
> Whom! Whom! not Who!
> There actually was a great Chinese actor named
>   Wang Whom
> who immigrated to the United States in the
>   mid-nineteenth century
> and found fame and fortune in the theaters of San
>   Francisco
> due mainly to his ability to allow his head to detach
> from his body and float up and disappear into the
>   dark
> The curtain would close to great applause
> and when it opened again his head was back
> but his body was in two halves split right down the
>   middle…

Is this not also a prose poem? Or do we need another category for this type of poem?

*

What is sound poetry? All poetry involves sound, I'm tempted to say, but then the moment I say this I start to think of exceptions. Joan Brossa's visual poems, or his poem-objects, do not involve sound, and I am tempted to think of them therefore as soundless poetry. One of these is hanging on the wall to my left as I make these notes: it is a screen print of a giant red S measuring 53cm x 22cm, with the tail of a fish entering the S bottom left and exiting (the head) top right. You can read this poem as articulating something about letters and objects – the way in which the letter S and the word 'fish', at least in English, are inextricably entwined (as they are in Catalan: peixos) – but you can't read it out loud. It remains silent. And yet, even here, sound becomes an absent-presence: and the more the eye concentrates on the red S the more noisy the poem becomes. The S is like the blood of the fish seeping onto a fishmonger's marble slab as it is split in two by a knife; or I hear the whoosh of the fish in the water as it darts about to avoid a predator, now in one place, now – whoosh! – in another. The absence of noise multiples noise; the soundless poem metamorphoses – and this, after all, is the theme of the poem on one level, where a letter metamorphoses into a fish – into a poem that is full of noises if we open our ears.

So perhaps, after all, it isn't all that far from the truth to say that all poetry involves sound, with the proviso that this sound might not always be heard. It might be missed, it might be mis-heard – and this 'missing' is something I would also say is characteristic of much poetry – when we read poems, or when I read poems, I often *miss* something, which is why we read poems again, why they don't disclose all their meanings, all their resonances, all their sonic resources, to us at once.

*

Imagine a poetry editor who is clean-shaven, smartly dressed, who believes in democracy, who has leftist leanings, who has turned his back on modernism in all forms, who believes that versioning ancient poetries is cultural appropriation. If this editor, rather than Ezra Pound, had been the first to set eyes on the manuscript of *The Waste Land*, that poem would have looked very different today. It might have begun like this:

> First we had a couple of feelers down at Tom's place,
> There was old Tom, boiled to the eyes, blind,
> (Don't you remember that time after the dance,
> Top hats and all, we and Silk Hat Harry,
> And old Tom took us behind, brought out his bottle
>   of fizz,
> With old Jane, Tom's wife; and we got Joe to sing
> "I'm proud of all the Irish blood that's in me,
> "There's not a man can say a word agin me").
> Then we had dinner in good form, and a couple of
>   Bengal lights.
> We got into the show, up in Row A,
> I tried to put my foot in the drum, and didn't the girl
>   squeal,
> She never did take to me, a nice guy – but rough;
> The next thing we were out in the street, Oh it was

cold!
When will you be good? Blew in to the Opera
    Exchange,
Sopped up some gin, sat in to the cork game,
Mr. Fay was there singing "The Maid of the Mill";
Then we thought we'd breeze along and take a walk.
Then we lost Steve.

Bibliography

Ashbery, John, *Houseboat Days* (London: Penguin, 1977).
Dickinson, Emily, *The Gorgeous Nothings*, Marta L. Werner and Jen Bervin (New York: Christine Burgin/New Directions, 2013).
Eliot, T.S., *The Waste Land: A Facsimile and Transcript of the Original Drafts* (London: Faber and Faber, 1971).
Malinovski, Pejk, *Poetry Texas* (London: Falling Tree Productions, 2012) *https://soundcloud.com/fallingtreeproductions/poetry-texas.*
Mallarmé, Stéphane, *Correspondance,* ed. Bertrand Marchal (Paris: Gallimard, 1995).
Métail, Michèle, *Identikits*, transl. Philip Terry (New York: Black Square Editions, 2021).
Noel-Tod, Jeremy (ed.), *The Penguin Book of the Prose Poem* (London: Penguin, 2019).
Padgett, Ron, *Collected Poems* (New York: Coffee House Press, 2013).
Spicer, Jack, *My Vocabulary Did This to Me: The Collected Poetry of Jack Spicer*, ed. Peter Gizzi and Kevin Killian (Middletown: Wesleyan University Press, 2008).
Valéry, Paul, *Poèmes et Petits poèmes abstraits, Poésie, Ego scriptor,* ed. Judith Robinson-Valéry (Paris: Gallimard, 1992).

Two Poems

PARWANA FAYYAZ

City of Ghosts

In the mountains, like humans the visible ghosts
Found refuge in their cells.
In caves, they made their homes.
Replaced the Buddha statues, close to the flowing river,
They remained mortal.

The invisible ones settle above each
Man's mind – like a cloud.
They drink the only river.
Resting above the tulips, they hunt men and then
    women.
Wasteland after wasteland,
They conquer.

Like a bird, they descend.
From caves to plains – mountains to rivers,
All build their one home.

Together – men wearing Kalashnikovs on their
    shoulders,
Women, bending the flour into dough.
Haunting, ethereal, another city is born
Visible only to the dead ones.
As for the living, we run.

A City Silenced

A drifter's melody roams Kabul city.
Smoke over smoke looks like some mountains of rocks.

It is just a mid-day habit but
At twilight, the centuries-old women rise from the
    earth.

They walk through the night,
With the dancing wind and the swirling dust.

These women roam with no notebooks
But ask for coal-ash for their pens.

Their meeting place is unknown –
Fallen into the fort walls of history.

Streets without their companions.
There is no clean throat to sing the song of the night.

Attar's *tarab* joy fades away for a moment.
Rumi's *tasawf* praising words bewilder.

Hafez's *ghazal* poems echo in invisibility.
Jami's *kalam* speech is suspended.

The cries of the tall grasses meet the black clouds,
And the black clouds meet the tempest.

The rivers stop flowing,
The little fish begin to bathe, at last, in the swirling
    dust.

In dust they fall, in dust they feel, in dust, they float.

Then with dust they descend, like Khayyam laments.

The last chamber of smoke dies.
The lanes of my city darken again,
Thickening and choking on themselves.

Did I not say, not to go there?
Rumi advises. We are told to be lost in the Call.

And to remember God so much that we are forgotten.
I see God is forgotten.

And both the caller and called are fully present.
Rumi vanishes into the smoky lanes.

Everyone else disappears.
Lampshades are broken. All alone.
The city rests in darkness.

Under the silver moon and in their silent songs,
The centuries-old women reappear in their half-selves.

They knock on each locked door – door to door – made
    of whims.
At dawn, they return to their tombs.

The echoes of their unheard songs disappear,
Leaving this city of mine faded and silent.

For its women are long silenced.
In the light, they sleep. In the dark, their bodies
Restlessly search for a world that never existed.

Hart Crane, Life among the Magazines

DON SHARE

If you go to Cleveland, Ohio, you'll discover that Hart Crane's house has vanished; a stubby cenotaph marks the spot. Nearby, at a local university, there's a landlocked statue of him, a singularly inadequate monument to a poet of the waters who met his fate at sea. Does he live on in critical conversations, at least? Ange Mlinko, for instance, writing recently on Frank O'Hara in the *London Review of Books*, noted that 'Among the young poets at Harvard, lines were drawn between Auden and Yeats, and Stevens and Eliot, with O'Hara and Ashbery championing the underdogs Auden and Stevens'. The latter hold their sway even now, but post-Derek Walcott (who always talked about him), post-William Logan (who has always

denigrated him), you seldom hear poets, especially younger ones, discuss Hart Crane in any depth. The world has changed, is always changing, but Crane, as ever, remains an elusive – even problematic – figure. So where might we find him now?

Since his tragic early death, he's been enshrined in two good editions of his collected poems, and then again in the authoritative Library of America series, but while living he was mainly to be found in the pages of contemporary literary journals. No doubt those Harvard poets were reading, and aspiring to be published in, many of the same ones Crane had; and they'd have met him in those pages. But Crane was among the first generations of

American poets to seek this particular path to success. The US has no Pantheon, but it does have litmags, lots of them. As Francesca Bratton points out in her lucid and illuminating study, *Visionary Company: Hart Crane and Modernist Periodical*, 'during his sixteen-year career, Crane amassed 109 publications in 26 journals' – which she calls a 'roll call of transatlantic periodicals', culminating in just two published books, plus a last, posthumous collection. And we're not just talking about *Poetry*, *The Dial*, *The New Republic* and *Saturday Review*, let alone well-known avant-garde journals like *Broom*, *Secession* and *transition* – but also the likes of *Bruno's Weekly*, *Bruno's Bohemia*, *Gargoyle* and *The Pagan*, less-remembered Greenwich Village magazines in which Crane's writing career actually started. Crane first read these journals in a Cleveland bookstore before he left what he called the 'hell of the Midwest' for New York City.

As it happens, nineteen-year-old Crane came to live in the Village himself, right above the offices of *The Little Review* of all places. Describing his bohemian beginnings there, Britton explains that far from being merely obscure and coterie-driven, the Village was a nexus and crucible of 'modernist transnationalism', whose periodicals cut across not only national but generational and gender boundaries. While living there, Crane appeared seventeen times (20 percent of his total publications, Britton calculates) in Joseph Kling's *The Pagan* alone until, receiving a rejection, he contemptuously cut his ties to the magazine. (The fury of the spurned submitter is a well-known and continuing phenomenon). Crane eventually moved out of the Village and away from its proto-Decadent influences; the fin de siècle/Imagist style poems that constitute his juvenilia, published in *Bruno's* and *The Pagan* would be excluded from his first published book, *White Buildings* (1926). Bratton nevertheless locates in Bruno's two journals a queer aesthetic, encoded, necessarily given the repressiveness of the Comstock era, in Wildean influences that were critical to Crane's artistic development. Bratton establishes not only Crane's emergence as a modernist poet with, as the poet himself joked, 'a little toenail' stuck in the nineteenth century, but the bigger, and complex, scene in which he developed. *Bruno's Weekly*, for instance, regularly reviewed (or mocked) other journals, and it's bracing to learn that Ezra Pound, in an irritated letter to Crane about where to send poems, thought the young poet's work (which he disliked) could go to one of them, *Contemporary Verse*, where it would, in the maestro's words, complement its 'consummate milk pudding milieu'.

One of the most useful points Bratton makes is that in contrast to the 'received history' and 'propaganda and myth-making' that claims the Imagists were breaking with their predecessors, literary magazines of this period highlighted a diverse and assimilative group of poets whose experimentation 'coalesced modern trends with those of the fin de siècle'. She amusingly demonstrates this in Crane's work by using an anthology of nineteenth-century poetry as a 'concordance' to correlate the vocabulary, images and tropes of his early poems with those of the Decadent poets, Wilde most of all. She also discusses borrowings from Mallarmé, Baudelaire and Apollinaire, as well as echoes of Laforgue, lest we think

this process limited to Anglo-Americans. As the Janus-like Crane surprisingly exclaimed in a 1923 letter: 'God DAMN this constant nostalgia for something always "new"'.

As Crane moved away from his early Village-based aesthetic, he moved towards journals and readers situated farther afield, appearing, in the early 1920s, in the *Double Dealer* (New Orleans), *The Fugitive* (Nashville, through which he meets Allen Tate) and cutting-edge magazines such as *The Dial* (Chicago, then New York), *Secession* (founded in Paris), *Gargoyle* (also Paris), *Broom: An International Magazine of the Arts* (founded in Rome, later edited from Paris), *S4N* (Massachusetts) and Eugene Jolas's *transition* (Paris). In this fertile decade, the machine age – as well as surrealist techniques of collage and juxtaposition – decisively and crucially enter his poetry. In his 1925 essay 'General Aims and Theories', he proclaims his intention to 'embody in modern terms (words, symbols, metaphors) a contemporary approximation to an ancient culture or mythology'. At the same time, Bratton argues, Crane began to realize ways in which periodical publishing itself 'might become part of a poem's form'. Having moved beyond his early work, this insight freed him to publish sections of his longer poems separately, 'with the parts functioning independently' – reserving whole, reassembled sequences for his ambitious second book, *The Bridge*. Bratton makes this case in detail, and includes a revealing chart tabulating Crane's journal submissions and publications, complete with the names of editors and information about rejections and even print runs – a feature as useful to her case that 'editing is a creative-critical practice' as it is novel.

As Bratton also shows, the 'fragmentary publication [of poems in *The Bridge*] conditioned its immediate reception', resulting in critical accusations of incoherence that still resound today. Moreover, it's also at this time that Crane meets what she describes as a homophobic 'critical opprobrium', e.g., Yvor Winters's influential equation of Crane's homosexuality with decadence and indiscipline, and Marianne Moore, as editor of *The Dial*, infamously retitling and cutting 'The Wine Menagerie' from forty-nine to eighteen lines on similar grounds to Winters (though to be fair, she cut her own poems down to size, too, such as 'Poetry' – from thirty-two to three lines). Moreover, as his famous published exchanges with *Poetry*'s editor Harriet Monroe about 'At Melville's Tomb' proved, his developing notion of the 'logic of metaphor' (exemplified in, to use Bratton's examples, 'metallic paradises' to mean high-rise buildings, and 'chairing strings' for the cables of the Brooklyn Bridge) – informed as it was by his readings in proto-Surrealist and avant-grade journals – would not be convincing, or even coherent, to everyone. Bratton argues that Crane's 'allusive gestures' and associative processes demonstrate that 'the wellspring of work that would constitute *The Bridge* was Crane's queer poetics' – meaning that a great deal of the critical thinking hostile to his work constitutes a hostility to expressions of queerness in his work. What ties Bratton's arguments together is her contention that 'Crane elides distinctions between textual and erotic bodies'. In any case, as Matthew Josephson, a fellow poet (and an editor at *Broom* and *transition*), put it, 'All of the drama of Hart's turbulent personality was there in the strange images of those verses'. Crane's path to what Bratton calls his American Futurism was not going to be an easy one.

Visionary Company is an academic book, but it reads better than most and can profitably be enjoyed by anyone interested in Crane's work, periodical culture, modernism, or all of these. It's impeccably documented and draws capaciously from a wide variety of sources. With every page the reader shares the rewards of Bratton's trawling through files and folders in dusty archives to bring this all to life again – and Crane himself, too. A key discovery is her finding of 'Nopal', a 'lost fragment from Crane's planned (but unrealized) Mexican epic', which sheds light on what Crane might have done beyond the Key West poems that make up his unfinished, final book manuscript. A smaller but worthwhile discovery is that Crane published an essay defending *Secession* against Amy Lowell under the pseudonym Religious Gunman – taken from a phrase in 'For the Marriage of Faustus and Helen'.

Bratton is an astute researcher, but happily also a gifted critic. Especially useful is her sharp, perspicuous examination of Crane's early, pre-book work, correlating these less well-known poems with what he was reading, as well as with his own later poetry. Importantly, she argues that accusations of failure and incoherence in *The Bridge* and other works rest on a category error 'embedded in narratives of Crane's poetry' that ignores the material significance of his work's fragmentary magazine publication history. *The Bridge* 'finds its form through dissemination and reconstitution via literary magazines', and that form is more like a 'collaged, Cubist' work than linear narrative or epic. Her argument that periodical publication constitutes form – that 'material and aesthetic forms work in tandem' may or may not convince everyone to read Crane's work differently (do Crane's idiosyncrasies require such an elaborate defense?), but it is indisputably useful to see him in this new light. And Bratton succeeds in showing the ways in which 'periodicals bear the traces of intimacies between individuals, collectives, sub-groups and coteries', and above all that Crane's poetry was shaped by the 'shifting communities' of magazine culture.

In the end, Crane graduated from the little magazines to publication (as well as attacks in) the 'smart' larger-circulation ones, with poems appearing in *The Saturday Review*, *The New Republic* and *The Nation*. There had always been a tension between avant-garde writing, intelligible only to a small, select audience, and its inexorable appearance in mainstream outlets. What Crane's literary career would have looked like had he lived longer is anyone's guess, but one can reasonably conclude from Bratton's book that Crane was in, though not of, the interrelated publishing coteries and communities of his time. (She even posits that a 'coterie context' can help us understand his notorious cannibalization of Samuel Greenberg's poems.) Crane, the man as well as the poet, can seem elusive – but with Bratton as our guide he seems more grounded (and in 'visionary company') than we may have realised, yet as imaginatively soaring as ever. She is right to establish that where we can find Hart Crane is in the pages of journals that first presented his work. The 'real-time argumentative literary culture of periodicals' still exists today, of course, shaping the contours of poetry and leaving its traces in the pages of literary magazines just as it did in Crane's day.

Three Poems

COLM TÓIBÍN

Electric Ireland

The pavement on Pembroke Street,
The flattened chewing-gum, the damp
Remnant of last night's rain on the slabs
Of concrete. And the postman,
Seeing me on the street, hands me
Two books in jiffy-bags –
Leland Bardwell's stories
And Billy O'Callaghan's first novel –
And also two ordinary envelopes,
One containing an ESB bill (or a bill,
From Electric Ireland, the ESB's new name),
The other a parking permit from the City Council
That covers two years, as the last disc did,
The one that is now about to expire.

A United Ireland

And someone is sure that they see,
As dawn light comes over Slieve Gullion and Cave Hill,
The unforgiven ones, the Shankill Butchers,
And the IRA men who did Kingsmill, Enniskillen and Omagh,
Bare their teeth in misery as smilers start to read the news.
A bevy of Fianna Fail princesses go shopping in Jonesborough.
O'Donovan Rossa is driving south in an old Volkswagen.
I think the IRA Army Council is really running the country
But at least they'll do something about housing.
The Dáil is addressed by Maire Comerford and Mrs. Pearse
Who sings *In Mountjoy Jail* until someone tells her
The wrong dead patriot, and then she begins to snarl
Lord, thou art hard on mothers to all concerned.
Dowager Lady Brookborough has finally written a novel,
Serialized on the radio by Stephen Rea.
At the end of each chapter, we howl with laughter
The ad for the series goes, to music by Scullion.
Kerry for the cup! Hilda O'Malley appeals for calm.
Fortinbras O'Fee moves south. Conor Cruise O'Brien
Warns against prevarication in all its guises.
But it is too late. *Ita Missa*. The dead are on the march.
No one can stop them: Andy Tyree, for example,
And Ronnie Bunting and Muriel MacDonagh and then there are
Some Fenian widows and the relatives of 1916
Who want pensions and places in the front row.
You can take all the tea in China, you can take it
To the island. John A. Murphy says that this new crowd
Lack the integrity of the old crowd. Electoral Mandate
Is climbing up the charts, way ahead of Robin Dudley Edwards.
Help, help, Desmond has fallen, Dudley whines
As Desmond Williams crosses from Hartigan's to Hourigan's.
And all the dead Fine Gaelers march on, march on:
John A. Costello, James Dillon, Gerry L'Estrange
With sad minor members of the SDLP.
Europe sends euros. *What we need are guns,*
For fuck's sake, and answers to our prayers,
Hear us on the ground of our beseeching.
And the old ships: the Asgard, the Eksund, the Marita Ann
Sailing frantically around the seven oceans.
I dreamed last night that Ireland was a *spéarbhean* –
Called Aisling or Emer or Mary McAleese –
And I wake to find that Ireland is not merely Gaelic
But free as well until I find my compass gone askew
Somewhere near Askeaton and I cannot tell in what direction
The convoys are moving. I only know that Ireland
Is one at last, as God wished. *We are facing the future*
With a newly-found confidence and optimism. I am driving
Towards you, my love, but I might first see what the story is
In Armagh, or Strabane, or Lisburn, or the towns beyond.

Some Say the Heart

In Houston Texas I was put sitting beside a heart surgeon,
An elderly fellow, slow-talking, cheerful, a lover of Yeats
So that often, he told me in a Texan drawl, as he poked
A scalpel into an artery or a valve, he would invoke Father Gilligan
Or intone *when you are old and grey and full of sleep.*

Shoving in stents, it struck me, now all the rage,
Must be easier than doing bypasses, once bloody and long.
But I phrased my thoughts on cardiology more politely,
Asking the doctor if one heart much resembled another
When you get to view them in that raw and open state.

I make artificial hearts, he said. With plastic? I asked,
Incredulous. More or less, he replied. And what do you
Use instead of blood, I enquired. No. He became almost sad
As well as serious. No, we still use blood. You cannot do
Without blood. But you – or anyone – can live without a pulse.

The hearts we make do not have a pump. There is no actual
Need for blood to pump. It is the pumping, among other things,
That wears out the heart and weakens veins and arteries.
Our patients have no pulse. Their bloods flows and flows
In a way that is orderly, rational, sane and pure.

In all your digging and cutting, I asked, in all the squelch
That lies within the human breast, did you ever see the soul,
Or even some fleeting trace of it, or hear a sough, a sigh
That hinted at a persistent presence inside bones and flesh?
The doctor grinned in approval. Now we are talking, he said,

But, believe me, there is only the body; that is the truth.
Nothing hides when you part the breast. What you see
Is all there is. That is why I like having poems to hand
As I saw and cut open. The body is dull, predictable.
It is a relief to hear about trees, their autumn beauty.

The doctor's eyes were full of mischief. He was an alchemist,
Daring me to ask him: since the pulse has gone the way
Of all flesh, what will we abolish next: rivers perhaps,
Libraries, rain; laws; diuretics, the stethoscope;
Pain, memories? What about the Texan drawl?

No, he said, sipping his wine, looking around the room,
Whatever happens to the heart, whatever more we can do
To prolong life, the drawl will remain. What we have killed
Is heartbeat, but it was never really needed.
It is like candlelight or the horse-drawn carriage.

Last week, he went on, I replaced the diseased heart of a man
With a heart I fashioned in a workshop. With no pulse at all,
The man was ready to imagine a future, asking for his phone,
Remembering those he must call, as love
Came back, flowing through him, regular, unmetred, deep.

The old surgeon smiled in satisfaction at the thought of this.
To keep people alive, he said, that is the whole point.
Who cares what the heart is made of? Who cares about the soul?
I care about the brightening glance, the hand, the touch,
And I love the words: transplant; artificial; unstressed flow.

Three Essays

LUTZ SEILER

Translated by Martyn Crucefix

Babelsberg

Brief Thoughts on Ernst Meister

Potsdam-Babelsberg is the name of the place where my then five-year-old daughter would go for ballet lessons. Twice a week, I took her there to the dance studio. The room, where the girls practised classical ballet steps to the accompaniment of music, had a large mirror at one end, beyond which there was a smaller, cramped room where their relatives – mostly mothers or grandmothers – sat on black chairs with green velvet cushions, anxiously watching the progress of their ballerinas. The mirror was see-through from that side. There, behind the mirror, with Tchaikovsky blaring from a cassette recorder and the dance teacher's instructions ringing in my ears, I balanced a book on my knees: its title was *Zahlen und Figuren* (Numbers and Figures), one of the volumes in the Rimbaud Press's Ernst Meister edition. In my notebook, dated 28 November, 1996, it says, 'get hold of ernst meister' – though there is no indication where the idea had come from. Two months later, there I was, sitting behind the mirror, by turns reading and making notes, then glancing up to watch my daughter starting sequences over and over again, her first laborious steps in the art of dance, and then I would turn back to reading Ernst Meister's poem: 'It is the walking, the way / and nothing more'. This is the opening of *Numbers and Figures*, though for some reason, at that moment, I was dipping into the book from back to front. Towards the end of the book, I had read:

> And within the circle,
> the killing, yet siesta in the garden,
> ice-skating elsewhere,
> a common,
> enduring, if not
> homely
> light, really
> astonishing.

Or a little earlier in the book: 'As for us, never at ease. / Too much is possessed by death.' Or: 'The unsyllabled / goodnight / of the world' and, still further back: 'A dead man / already forgotten / has wrapped himself in gold leaf ' – my favourite lines from a poem which, as I have since discovered, Meister wrote after walking round a graveyard with Walter Höllerer. In these poems, published in 1958, death is already the leitmotif of Meister's work: 'Old crosses / and a new art'. And when I had worked my way back to the very beginning of the book,

set down there, as I have said, I read: 'It is the walking, the way / and nothing more'. On the far side of the mirror, my daughter, incredibly, was practicing a handstand, or at the least, was bravely flinging her legs up into the air.

Walking and footsteps had been a theme in my own work around that time, and I had been gathering material on the subject. When I had added Meister's lines, I realised I already had a similar, almost identical passage on the subject of walking in my notes. It was something I had earlier taken from a poem by Nicolas Born in which he seemed, just a few years later, to be responding to Meister's poem: 'It is the walking – no headway'. Then I saw further correspondences between Meister's lines and some of the other phrases and images I had collected, such as between the deliberate bodily confusion in the 'First Epistle to the Corinthians' ('Now if the foot should say, because I am not a hand' etc.) and the confusions in Meister's first great book, *Ausstellung* (Exhibition): 'The man crossing his yellow legs as he sleeps. / Kneels his knees down into his mouth'. And while trying to imagine the fantastical walking of this poet from Hagen, his stride, his demeanour, I came across his author photograph at the front of the book, facing the title page. An old-fashioned portrait, I thought: studiedly posed, exaggerated in its seriousness, an almost Rilkean image of contemplation, yet not languid, or weak, but with all its energy focused on a point, beyond the picture, that remained invisible.

I looked at the image, the neat clothes, the pipe and tobacco tin on the table, the head propped on the hand: as an observer, you were not being invited into this picture. Rather it suggested a closed relationship between the author and whatever it was that remained unseen. It was a proud display that quite consciously – and not without a touch of pathos – gestured towards a wholly independent, autonomous meaning.

Nowadays writers smile in their author photographs, frequently they laugh, often heartily, revealing amazingly good teeth as if to say how comfortable and well-groomed life can be, even for a writer. If an author is not already grinning into the camera of his or her own volition, experienced photographers will soon ask if, perhaps, they couldn't look a little more friendly. Novice authors might want to present a face more appropriate to their text, or at least one that doesn't wholly undermine it. But then it is especially such inexperienced authors who will encounter a novice photographer, who immediately harangues them with: 'Give me a smile!' or 'How about a laugh?'

In contrast, Ernst Meister never laughs in the pictures which we designate as author photographs. In these portraits, the author represents his text. In these images, it is the same as in the poems: Meister keeps his life shut away, with an unconcealed seriousness and, something become increasingly rare in this context, a sense of what might be called dignity. These author images suggest what the poems have to say: 'this is mine'. In the case of Meister, this 'mine' is often interpreted as hermetic: as if any author were capable – as poetic debate often tends to suggest – of doing anything other than whatever is really his own. You might say: the poem – in being at one with the writer's life – is something that necessarily asserts itself, that it is the writer's own song.

(2003)

In the Anchor Jar

In writing, there are always those moments when you cannot make progress. Days when you pace round the room endlessly, around the material, when in actual fact you are circling yourself, repeatedly mouthing something aloud, to your ear, only to hear the same thing over and over again: it's not right. A dervish squats on the voice and constricts it. For as long as it takes, until the utterance is right, then he grows animated, he adds his part, that ineffable something to the whole, and on both sides the feeling of gratitude is great. As great as the despair when things are not working out.

One evening, about eight years ago, when I had been similarly stymied for a while and was close to despair, I took myself down to the cellar. It may have been that I was already a bit disorientated, at any rate exhausted, like a creature that has spent too long circling an invisible prey. I explored the shelves in the semi-darkness and eventually found what I was looking for: a few empty glass jars covered in coal dust. When I had washed them off, I could see the maritime symbol they carried on the lid and the lettering of an old, comforting name: they were ANCHOR jars. Ribbed glass jars made by the Anchor company in Saxony – jars that had been used and handed down in my family for several generations. Back at my desk, I took a pair of scissors and, without a moment's hesitation, carefully started to cut up my drafts. I cut right through verses and stanzas, seldom leaving many lines together, scissoring words or groups of words from the page. And it felt good, a positive feeling, making good progress, and so I also cut up earlier manuscripts and papers that had been languishing in a drawer and I filled my Anchor jars with them. Then I sealed them up. I attached a length of adhesive tape as a label and dated the jars with the year and the season: *Autumn 1996*. I had preserved them.

At the time, I did not feel the least inclination to account for such a bizarre action. That only changed when I broke open my jars in the summer of 2003 and I had to ask myself: why had writing turned to preserving that evening? Why this rather helpless resort to an old, unliterary process?

Making preserves: every year there was a fruit harvest that got completely out of hand. For days on end, over-supply and stockpiling round the hearth in the steam-filled utility kitchen and, in front of it, the hurriedly gathered outlines of several familiar shapes. On the big burners stood the preserving pans, which, with thermometers protruding from their lids like antennae, looked like nothing so much as spaceships ready to launch. From my vantage point at the kitchen table, my command centre, I viewed these ships' failure to achieve lift off with a critical eye. It seemed perfectly possible they might explode at any moment. In what was called a 'good year' there was a deluge from the garden that quite swamped us. I can still hear, 'There's too much,' or 'I can't manage it', then a groaning from the vaulted cellar, where the filled jars were being stacked, no longer just on shelves, but along passageways and on the stone steps that led directly into the cellar from the kitchen. From the start, it seemed inconceivable that all this produce would ever be consumed. But to give up, to abandon something to decay, that was simply out of the question. On the contrary, additional jars, rubber bands and clips were hastily procured and at long last, several days later, the invasion had finally been contained and dispatched into the Anchor jars of that particular vintage, examples of which, simply due to the sheer numbers, would still be turning up in the backs of cupboards decades later, the fruit covered with a thin, chalky crust that was claimed not to be mould and so no reason not to consume it. What I really felt about this I only came across later in the cellar poem, 'Down There', by W.H. Auden: 'Encrust with years of clammy grime, the lair, maybe, / Of creepy-crawlies or a ghost'.

It was only in the context of her war experiences, the anxieties associated with them, that I could make much sense of my grandmother's talk after this onslaught – and even in her exhaustion – of 'the blessing of fruit that keeps on giving'. No – no such corresponding hardship had been the precursor to my writing crisis. And no, I did not consider my scribblings as 'giving', quite the contrary. Yet, even in the midst of my distress, I had impulsively turned to just this practice, from my own upbringing, with which a seemingly impossible circumstance might be managed via a mechanical process. And why should I not think of my jars as part of the storehouse of technical aids about which Edgar Allan Poe writes in his *Philosophy of Composition*. With the help of these jars, I had not merely set my material aside, I had transposed it in time.

A preserve retains juice and hence freshness, yet everyone knows preserves do not taste like the original fruit. Between the fruit and the jar that is later opened comes the method, the process and – above all – time. The preserved fruit tastes of time. Today I would say that the best thing about a poem when you recite it to yourself is that it tastes of time. Working on the poem amounts to an investment of time, in the proper sense of the word. The result is the poem's temporal power, which in turn is essential for the potency of its imagery. It is not a question of any specific verb tense: its fascination is with the passage of time. In my work on a poem, for example, this means delving into the past for the very moment, for the first stirrings of the poem, the moment of its inception. Working with this particular, non-paraphraseable moment is difficult: on the one hand, it must be preserved and, if I succeed in doing this, it will emerge, intact, in the final version as a kind of infant form of the poem. Despite all the painstaking and tiresome labour, it is precisely from this that the completed poem will draw an essential part of its power. The other requirement, as I have said, is the vertical work, revealing the layers of time within which this poem's core is embedded, the search for the lines of its magnetic field across history, biography or technology.

Today, when I think back to the sense of pleasure that I experienced in cutting up my manuscripts, I understand things more clearly. Apart from the satisfaction that the aggressive, purely destructive aspects of this action might have yielded, there must have been a vague expectation, in the depths of my despair, that what I was doing would not only liberate the present, but also create the future. I was transposing my material into an 'ideal now' in the future, a forthcoming present of wonderful writing moments that would be elicited by this material when I could re-encounter it as if new – moments of awakening, of grasping before understanding, which the poem needs in order to be a poem: in those jars lay dreams of my future writing.

Anchor jars – in some ways they seem the opposite of a message in a bottle. In 1958, on receiving the Bremen Literature Prize, Paul Celan described the poem as a message in a bottle. An Anchor jar and a message in a bottle: both are receptacles with a maritime association, yet their movements, their locations, their histories are quite different. In the case of the message in a bottle, there is a forsakenness, a sense of something having been lost on both sides, both sender and recipient are afflicted by it.

Doubts about the addressee, even about the legitimacy of contemplating an addressee, and the hope – more or less besieged by these doubts – for some specific impact resulting from the poem and its language: nowadays, it seems to me, these ideas have been absorbed into the act of writing itself, they have become an element of the self-reflection involved in the process of writing. Doubt: the author no longer needs to propose it, there is hardly any reason for him to address this difficult subject in any extra-literary way. When I write today, from the outset I can no longer assume the role of a self-evident speaker of a message destined for an audience. This is a definitive shift in the author's disposition that has an impact not only on his methods but also on the text he writes. A message in a bottle and an Anchor jar – instead of speaking in vague terms about the 'author', perhaps I would do better to focus on the receptacles, because it is only at first sight that the differences between them predominate. With both these vessels, time is gained, time is invested. The Anchor jar, with its fragments, can then perhaps be viewed as an experiment in the deferral of the promise implied in the image of a message in a bottle on its way. Or to put it

another way: as a message in a bottle, these Anchor jars were *en route* into my own writing. Both these vessels serve to transform the failures of the present, by way of an old technology, into a hope for the future. And in this way, the present becomes more manageable, and the work can also proceed as, eventually, it did in my own case.

In cutting up and preserving my manuscripts (without boiling them, of course) there certainly lay my wishful thinking to return language to the status of matter, a poetic raw material, treating it, if such a thing is possible, as a kind of natural substance. At first glance, my picking up the scissors might look brutal, but I only severed structure and I did not harm a single word in the process. Today I see the whole procedure more as an act of conservation, of precaution, also in the sense of laying up stores. Yet the process of preserving does not only represent a desire for conservation and a wish to return language to substance, it also represents the wish to seek out the particular place where it may be properly accommodated.

As a child, every day after school my job was to light the stove. Stove-ash-bucket-cellar-coal-stove: that was the orbit of those afternoons. It might take me an hour to re-emerge from the cellar. There was a numbingly sweet dead-mouse smell in the air and a bluish gleam of cyanide in the corners. The cellar sent me into dream states, states of ease and complete absence. Almost motionless, I stood with a candle in my hand (the electric light was broken) and cast light over the shelves, or better to say I eavesdropped on them. Behind me on the wall hung the huge baseboard of a model railway, beside me my great-grandmother's old tallboy cabinet, but before me were arrayed rows of preserves, a collection of museum proportions. Reading the jars, I made out the neatly inscribed adhesive tape, my mother's handwriting, or my grandmother's, occasionally an unfamiliar hand with dates that, to my childish imagination, referred to an inconceivably distant past. Perhaps this was my first reading in the passage of time. There was a silence that seemed to emanate from those dusty jars and to which I responded with a kind of muttering, something vocalised, a conversation with myself. A kind of primal scene, perhaps, in the story of one's own voice. The mute presence of these preserves, their organic immobility, stirred something in me, and I made inchoate sounds. At least I did until I reached the lower shelves with my candlelight, my reading light. There sat the jars containing meat and sausage, the archives of liver, blood and fat. Every year, on my grandfather's farm, we still slaughtered our own meat. The slaughter party meant: the child gripping the drumming limbs of the staked, panicking animal as the butcher applied the bolt gun to its head. Or: the child being asked to come hold the animal's intestines while they are rinsed over the sink, the child vomiting. He gets poured his first vodka, which he flings behind him, against the laundry room wall. So, there are things to smile about and, by way of consolation, one half of the much-coveted brain, which was said to have miraculous powers, and its little oily mass is already sizzling in the pan. Every year a slaughter day, every year new jars of black pudding, liver sausage, minced meat – for my entire childhood and youth, this is what filled my sandwiches. Home-butchered meats were precious and highly prized, but my problem with them was the lack of variety – though nothing as bad as Woyzeck's bean diet, of course. If you are what you eat, as we used to say, if I believed in this morphological short circuitry, then every time I went to fetch the coal, did I not have to fight off the thought, standing in front of those shelves, that I was staring into my own future, indeed catching a glimpse of myself in those jars? Driven by my writing crisis, I had clearly been determined to overcome the considerable levels of physical disgust that contemplating such preserves tended to produce in me. To see myself, not only provisioned with these jars, but also prepared, in the true sense of the word, I mean, to imagine myself in what was yet to come, that remained the crucial experience.

Everything is connected: an understanding of passing through time and of the power of time in the poem. A message in a bottle, an Anchor jar – vessels for the extraction of time. The desire for a substance-like state of language and, eventually, a place for its accommodation, its contemplation, ultimately a place for the creation of the poem, grounded, hushed, filled with absence. And when I look through my notebooks of this period, it becomes clear that my obsession with preserving as a literary technique went hand in hand with the discovery of material from my childhood, that is, the actual time of such preserving, of archiving moments that later appear timeless in the poem. In this sense, the point at which I got blocked on that particular occasion and at which I turned to scissors and cutting, marked a moment of change, a reorientation in my own writing.

So, at last, back to the jars. There were times when I picked them up, shook them and I could make out individual words through the ribbed glass. But mostly the jars just stood alongside notebooks; more recently they were hidden behind books on a shelf. Something happened over time. My writing had finally moved on and the promise that was preserved in those jars, or that I had taken to be in them, now seemed dubious. Sure, I had thought about it on occasions, but I had always refrained from opening the jars. Imperceptibly, their meaning had changed before my eyes. I had to admit to myself that now, instead of a promise, I sensed a kind of threat: vessels in which nothing more nor less than an old writing crisis had been preserved. Something to be kept locked away at all costs; at best, to be thought of as a symbol of coping with it. But as so often happens, curiosity and recklessness won the day and, seven years later, I opened the jars, though I first took the precaution of packing their contents, sight unseen, into several envelopes and stowing them in my luggage on my way to Los Angeles, where I was to spend the summer. To be honest, the outcome was oddly sobering. Beside a window that looked out across Santa Monica Bay, among the scattered bits of paper on my desk, there was, with hardly any exceptions, really nothing that had been forgotten. Over the course of the previous few years, almost every word, every connection, had been incorporated, in one way or another, into my poems. I had preserved; I had set aside, yet nothing had been lost to the writing, nothing had been lacking, nothing but time. In the Anchor jars, everything had taken its time: the words had taken their time till *their* text had emerged and I too had taken the time to find a belief in myself and in this voice.

(2004)

The Flute Player

'The Flute Player' was the only picture I had in my kitchen in Berlin, at Rykestraße 27, in the back-courtyard building. I had hung it on the wall above the kitchen workbench. This bench was where I wrote – my workshop is how I thought of it at the time. With its heavy, rusting steel frame and four-metre-long wooden boards, it almost filled the room. On top of the boards rested the slightly chipped marble top of an old dressing table and it was on this that I actually wrote, pleasingly cool to my forearms as I worked there in the summer. It was even better if I put my pen down, turned my arms and pressed my wrists to the stone; it was almost a shock, a delightful coolness that penetrated my blood, ran up my back, my neck, and rippled over my scalp, palpating my skull like a precious helmet, the contours of which were just tangible there beneath the skin. For a few moments, I sat transfixed. That was when my gaze would fall on the image of the flute player and what I wished for was to live a life like his, in that house, on that hilltop, overlooking other houses, in a light that fell benevolently on everything, a life that seemed to have achieved a perfect balance.

Since my school days, Rik Wouters's painting had been kept in a folder with other reproductions of images. Our 'art master' – rather a fancy phrase for someone giving art lessons in school – had handed each of us a folder and, during the course of the year, everyone was supposed to assemble their own little collection of examples of pictures from different periods. I had taken 'The Flute Player' to be the work of an Impressionist painter and, as far as I can remember, the art teacher never raised any objections. At the time, I neither knew who Rik Wouters was (I knew nothing of his short life), nor had I ever heard of Fauvism.

1990: all my travelling in that particular year took me to France, mostly to the south, to one of the villages of the Languedoc, in the department of Hérault. It was precisely here that I imagined my new life unfolding. I would sit and write in one of those stone-built, sunlit houses, the very sight of which filled me with such confidence. I would simply have to despatch poems to my publisher on a regular basis and, perhaps, write something on the side for a newspaper and come evening, slowly and contentedly, I would drive my battered Ford Escort through the little villages down to the coast. I would take a walk along the shore, have a drink, or perhaps I would drive on to Montpellier to meet P... Every conceivable complication (actually, which publisher? what newspaper?) and all foreseeable difficulties – the foreign language, P's husband – seemed insignificant to me at the time. It was simply that the sudden, still wholly unfamiliar, almost startling possibility of living a life elsewhere triggered in me the most marvellous fantasies. And what do we take fantasies to be? They are plans; in 1990, the South of France was my plan.

It was not only the Mediterranean setting of such a fantasy that I recognised in the picture of the flute player. More than that, it was the easy-going, yet composed and serious figure presented by the young man, that air of calm and contemplation that I yearned for when I sat at my workbench on Rykestraße. I admired his autonomy. The calm way in which he pursued his art by letting it be and hence becoming more at ease with it. How to achieve that? How to get there? What were the secret pathways? How did one cross over into this mode of focused absence that was a prerequisite of poetry?

But there were other occasions as well. When I would come home around five o'clock in the morning from the Assel – the bar where, after the currency union, I earned a living, making no more than seven marks an hour – and I made the mistake of heading into the kitchen, to my workbench, instead of going straight to bed. Then it happened that the southern radiance enveloping the flute man would strike me as artifice, as not real. Then

it was the black edges that caught my eye (the dark curtains to the left and right of the window) and the strange rigidity of his broad, angular tie which echoed the black of the curtains and hung from his neck like the heavy pendulum of a clock. Was it this perpendicular that dragged his gaze downwards? Had he put his flute down to listen to the noise of the machinery in his own chest, a sound he found difficult to reconcile with his music?

Then, there was no music from the flute, only silence filled the room. Only the sound of time. The man's silence was no accident, nor a blessing, rather, it was an attitude, a way of sustaining himself there in the sunshine, with patience, with humility – there was a moment at which I came to see the picture in this way.

For several years, Wouters's image, hanging over my workbench, was an important point of reference for me, a reassurance. The flute player who is not playing. The one who pauses and goes deeper into himself. Just as he was gazing at a sheet of paper, or a book, with his head bowed (and his eyes closed?), I could stare at his image as I sat there, with my forearms pressed to the cool marble slab (a pulse on the stone), and contemplate a promise made to the future.

(2006)

From the Archive

from *PNR* 170, Volume 32 Number 6, 2006

First

The consensus is you are reading
or were that day
the camera snapped you

in your half-world, a mothy flicker
evoking open-mouthed wonder in ours.

Whisper it through the walls, wee yin.
We have forgotten.

The secrets heard
when gravity first pulls
on the silvery shadow.

GERRY MCGRATH

more available at www.pnreview.co.uk

Two Poems

SARAH MNATZAGANIAN

In Jaffa, my grandmother Takouhi Zakarian

cut white cambric, pierced it with leaf shapes,
buttonholed raw edges and linked the widest spaces
with fine cotton rungs, and then embroidered flowers.

How many thousand stitches did she leave behind?
Was it her life's work to heal the frayed?

Over the heart and below each hip she cut a rectangle
and filled it with a grid, like the grille between harem
and house. She stitched deer, flowers, leaves.

When I wear the camisole I see my skin through the spaces
she left and feel her young, warm, ready for my grandfather.

Imagine him waiting to be acceptable to her, changing
himself, letting go of ghosts. I imagine the oasis of her,
waiting, embroidering messages of purity and faith.

The world makes way for people who know where they're going

(Poster in a West Jerusalem fashion store, 2017)

Where have the name stones gone from the old Nablus houses?
The names that told Nabulsis where they belong?

At night, huge fingers prised them from doorways to play
five-stones, teaching their children how to win.

Throw. Catch them on the back of your hand. Snatch them up.
The stones can't talk any more.

Should we keep a note of where our Jaffa house stood and give the key
to our children, although the house has gone?

*

There's a small lump of shrapnel behind my father's ear, the colour
of his greying hair. It sets off metal detectors in airports.

He doesn't know whose bomb exploded in the Armenian convent
where he was sheltering with his brother seventy three years ago.

They were catapulting small pieces of orange peel at empty rifle cartridges
when the bomb fell. Crochet hooks were used to excavate their flesh.

His skin has healed over metal it was never meant to harbour.
It's not the key to unlock his Palestinian past.

Three Poems

MAITHREYI KARNOOR

Distance Soup

I would trade some of the fondness
To reduce the distance
To skin deep
And still have enough leftover
For a lifetime of elevenses.

Dear heart, when you come home
I will make a bonfire of the finest poetry
                of love and longing
And heat you soup on it.

Reverberations of Loss

The day my cat died

I hoped they would stop the hammering

And the drilling in the flat below mine

For an hour.

They didn't.

The sun hadn't been up the past two days

And there was no hot water in the taps.

I found that the biryani take-away

From three days ago

Came with two complimentary tea candles.

It was *eid* the previous day.

The cold shower was softly lit;

I could not hear the silence in my eyes.

Skinny Dipping in Tiger Country

I think of the old world
(Of the love for love and art for art's sake)
Where death was mostly by hunger, anger, and the small things in between.
I am neither hungry nor angry
    I have enough
    I have had enough.

        I eat and drink and look out the window at the papayas on the tree
            Being slowly devoured by moths.

Comeuppance is a low hanging fruit
In tiger (tiger burning bright) country:

           Giveuppance, on the other hand, is inherited
           (Earned in rare cases)

Crown shyness of grafted mango trees forms a peninsula
Around the moon – full, new, and blood – that is known to send men
Raving and raging over the precipice
Even as moonblood continues to evade them.

Under this is the river (its pool a steady mercy)

           The distance between me and the nearest tiger is a function

                Of diminishing trees

          My nakedness is an erotic invite to nobody
            But polymorphously perverse leeches

      Courage is joy in a free country and madness in a tiger one
         Courage is calculated abandon
            Against the lack of love
      The willingness to learn a new word one syllable at a time
           In narrow nightlight
    Before pronouncing it aloud with acquired ease in broad daylight
        (Courage is a cowardly cartoon dog)

With a boulder stand, a jump, a plop
A rise to cries of delicious cold
Of one's own making,
I skinny dip
Inquilab zindabad [1]!

          Curious fish, furious moss, indignant stones, seditious water
           Watchful tree canopy, swooping kingfishers, listless frogs
               Tame geese and lustful peacocks
                 Rouse my skin-deep passions
        My state of undress is a state of mind in my mindless state

          The beer is chilled in the river
             I write drunk
             Edit in October.

1 Long live the revolution

Meeting Mr Lowry

after a poem by Sinéad Morrissey

MARK HAWORTH-BOOTH

1970 – the city
was scrubbing off soot, turning
its back-to-backs to rubble
and gradually receding from his paintings.
A pretty colleague ventured with me
to Mottram in Longendale.

He was large but bird-like,
a dark-suited stork –
quizzical movements of the head,
sharp eyes, unexpected:
when Sandra admired a picture
he immediately offered it to her.

Knowing her museum ethics,
she gave a gracious no
to the small painting of the sea –
empty, white and lonely –
and it stayed on his mantelpiece.
We wondered if this was a test or trick –

but Lowry warmed to us, it seems.
The curtains remained closed,
his clocks all ticked and he
became less guarded,
eventually inviting us to the sanctum
of his picture-hung bedroom.

A brass bedstead, on the walls
flame-haired women
in red pastel or chalk,
I think about a dozen –
all of them Rossettis,
Lowry's greatest prize.

We stood and looked and looked.
'Imagine being kissed
by those lips' he suddenly
exclaimed, pointing at a portrait
titled 'Reverie' – Jane Morris
by her lover, obsessed Rossetti.

Lowry proposed lunch
and we took the bus together
back to town from Greater Manchester.
'We'll find a soup kitchen',
he joked – but chose respectable
dining at the Midland Hotel.

Afterwards, the short walk

to the art gallery, our gallery
but also his, which he'd –
from early youth – frequented.
I remember how he gazed,
his tall figure statuesque,

at a six foot picture
titled *Astarte Syriaca*
by, of course, Rossetti –
an un-Christian Trinity
with Jane Morris in the centre
and two younger beauties

as angel-winged attendants,
one her daughter May,
both of them red-headed
and holding redder flames.
I watched for several minutes
as Lowry stood enraptured.

Was he lost in the waves of her hair,
Jane's lustrous *chevelure,*
or willing her slender fingers
to loosen the spangled girdle
with which they toy and the goddess
reveal her blinding nakedness?

Was he worshipping his muse,
an Oriental Venus
and early Aphrodite
for whom nothing is above
the one commandment to love –
rather than looking at a Rossetti?

He didn't paint like that –
no need, it had been done.
What Lowry did was paint
with unassuageable love
how people are uncommon,
how folk are and live

sometimes lonely as the sea.

*Note: I am indebted to Sandra Martin for adding
her memories to mine and writing 'An
unforgettable trip to The Elms – Lowry & the
Pre-Raphaelites', the Lowry Blog, 21 December
2018.*

John Lucas

In conversation with

RORY WATERMAN

RW: You've been running Shoestring Press since 1994. What are the biggest changes you've noticed in poetry publishing over the past three decades, and how have they affected the press?

JL: I need to go back to my student years at Reading university in the late 1950s, when I became friendly with John Wain. He had given up his lectureship and begun life as a freelance writer, but retained an interest in Reading University Press, which he'd helped to start. The Press concentrated on slim volumes of poetry, in editions of 150 copies, using good-quality paper. I started the Byron Press in 1965, soon after arriving in Nottingham, and made a point of seeking out Michael Kane, who taught typography at the city's art college, and Albert Haynes, an expert on matters typographic. So when I set up Shoestring, I thought I knew how to do it. But then came computers.

It seems to me that the big changes in the world of poetry publishing all occurred in the latter half of the 1990s, especially with the withdrawal of some larger presses from their earlier commitment to publish work by living poets, and the enlargement of the world of micro presses, whose work is often pretty shoddy. Moreover, in 1994, poets who submitted to the press had for the most part spent time – not infrequently long years – sending out work to magazines before putting together a book-length collection. But the proliferation of university Creative Writing courses meant that quite suddenly I was being inundated, or so it felt, with typescripts by very young writers who had been assured by their tutors that they were ready for their first book.

Weren't you involved in the establishment of Creative Writing programmes at Nottingham Trent University in the early 1990s?

No, I had nothing to do with setting up the CW course at NTU. I ran workshops at Reading and Nottingham but they were on a voluntary basis. At Reading, Ian Fletcher had shown me poems on stapled sheets by Gael Turnbull's Migrant Press that had been sent him from, I think, California, and I shamelessly borrowed Gael's format in order to start *Poetry Broadsheet*. This appeared every three weeks, printed poems by students and others, and we'd meet of an evening to subject the contributions to a grilling. Sometimes a visiting/vagrant poet might appear, led heaven knows how to us poor sods. Jon Silkin turned up on one occasion which led to blood on the carpet. Then in Nottingham I began *Poetry Programme*. Same format, same procedure, and a succession of student editors, including Malcolm Carson and Hugh Underhill, both of whom in due course became pub-

lished poets. Nottingham in the 1970s was blessed with a number of city pubs that had upper rooms you could hire cheaply for an evening, and the discussion meetings usually took place in one of those. As with Reading, they were lively, no holds barred occasions and led to the bruising of several egos. But I hope, and think, they encouraged critical engagement, made for better readers, and were of use to budding poets.

Don't university Creative Writing courses also encourage critical engagement, make for better readers, and serve a purpose for budding poets?

In 1961, when I began Poetry Broadsheet, Creative Writing wasn't so much as a twinkle in Malcolm Bradbury's eye. Philip Hobsbaum may have started his meetings in Belfast by then, though I do know that Derek Mahon went to one and never went back. In the 1950s G.S. Fraser had held evenings in his Chelsea flat where poets came to read and wrangle. Peter Porter told me these were often drunken affairs which might end in virtual brawls and that on one occasion Fraser 'threw' Edward Lucie Smith downstairs for insulting Paddy, George's wife. But I'm not aware of other such gatherings at that time.

I don't think you've answered the question.

No, you're right. Of course CW courses should encourage critical engagement, make for better readers, and serve a purpose for budding poets, but I have to say that the only times I've acted as an external examiner for such courses I've been taken aback by the fierceness with which tutors have defended (championed?) some pretty weak work. I can understand, I suppose, why it happens. There's bound to be a closer relationship between tutor and tutee than on conventional Eng. Lit. courses, and perhaps the tutor's own reputation may be thought to be at stake. Anyway, I might have been expecting too much. Besides, those occasions were at a time when CW courses were new(ish) and those responsible for them felt under institutional pressure to justify their existence.

Jo Dixon, whose debut collection, Purl*, you published in 2020, became interested in writing poetry on a Creative Writing MA, and most of the poems in that book were written for her PhD.*

I'm not sure what I can add to what you've told me, although I'm pleased to learn that she was awarded a PhD for her work. And I'm delighted that she's now working with Dutch poets in translating their work.

Please say more about the proliferation of 'shoddy' presses, as you described them earlier.

Poorly produced pamphlets, which now seem everywhere, appear to be calculated to disarm criticism, though they have the opposite effect on me. I'm a Morrisian socialist. 'Have nothing in your house you do not think useful or believe to be beautiful.' Much of the 'poetry' that comes my way is neither use nor ornament. There's far more of it than I ever encountered when for the best part of ten years during the 1980s and early 1990s I was poetry reviewer for the *New Statesman*. Or perhaps the great Derek Mahon, who was *de facto* the *Statesman*'s literary editor when I was invited to act as reviewer, simply binned it all. This is a brief answer because a longer one would take me well beyond the word limit you've set me. I will, though, say that while I can see the case for limited editions, and while I'd certainly make exceptions for work by decent poets who want to send out a few copies of poems they value to friends of theirs, much of what appears feels to be coyly offered as a glimpse of some protected species. 'Don't come too close. You may harm it.' Well, I'm with Voltaire. 'Ecrasez l'infame.' I was recently sent a pamphlet of 'radical' verse I was meant to admire. It was dreadful stuff. Inept rhymes, wonky syntax, dodgy scansion and (at best), little idea how to use stanza forms. Read and learn from Byron's savaging of Laureate Southey, especially his mocking of Southey's clumsy hexameters. ('Not one of all whose gouty feet would stir.') Write badly and you comfort the enemy.

How important is it to you, or to Shoestring, to nurture talent? You have published quite a few debut collections, often by poets who have established very solid reputations without being at all fashionable.

Very. I'm an interventionist editor. I want any book or pamphlet I publish to be as good as I can make it. Silk purses may be rare but sow's ears aren't encouraged. It's always a thrill to come across good work by a name new/unfamiliar to me and to be able to help the work. So yes, Nadine Brummer, Jo Dixon, Neil Fulwood, Roy Marshall and Robert Selby are among poets I'm delighted to have taken on. I'm also determined to do all I can to introduce to English readers work by non-English-speaking poets who ought to be known here. I have a Greek List, going back to Kalvos and Solomos (Greece's 'National Poet'), and including a number of moderns and contemporaries, especially, perhaps, Tasos Denegris, Karouzos, the great Katerina Anghelaki-Rooke, and Spiros Vrettos; there is a shorter but, I think, good Dutch list – Remco Campert – his translator, Donald Gardiner, won the Vondel Prize, which was a boost for the press, Miriam van Hee, and – a personal favourite – Toon Tellegen; and I make sure that the work is translated by writers who are themselves proven poets. These include the American/Greek Philip Ramp, Judith Wilkinson, whose versions of Tellegen I greatly value, and W.D. 'Bill' Jackson, Matthew Barton and Christine McNeill, all of whom have translated from the German of Heine, Rilke, etc. And I also publish work by poets from under the Southern Cross, several of whom have over the years become good friends, and all of whom ought to be known and read this side of the world. Among them are Adrian Caesar, Jan Owen, Andrew Sant, and Michael Wilding, novelist, short-story writer, biographer, critic, and sometime publisher.

Quite a few of the 'new' poets you mentioned earlier are not especially young, of course.

Yes, quite a few Shoestring poets are older women, most of whom came back to poetry, usually via writing groups, having left it behind once they finished at university. One told me that she felt the male poets she knew in her early years regarded women as items of decoration or bed warmers. I don't want to single out any of them for special mention, because I value them all, though I can't resist saying how thrilled I was the first time I heard Nadine Brummer read. It was at the launch of an anthology of Jewish women poets when a contributor from Cambridge, treating her audience as the great unwashed, told us, *inter alia*, that only idiots took George Steiner seriously, and that haiku was a Chinese poetic form. She then read some appallingly bad poems and sat down with a smirk of accomplishment. After which Nadine, with no introduction, stood and read poems that were the real thing.

I realise poetry isn't (quite!) only read by poets, but how important do you think it is for poets to read work from multiple languages?

Well, as MacNeice said, 'World is various, and more of it than we think'. In the mid-1970s, the Old Icelandic scholar Christine Fell came to work in Nottingham, and introduced me to Viking sagas. With her guidance, I produced for Dent/Everyman a version of *Egil's Saga*. The Rough Guide to Viking Culture is more or less as follows: Morning, take to the longboat, discover an island, slaughter the locals; afternoon, a spot of pillaging; evening, get legless. But the formal splendour of Viking poetry, because it's intended for recitation and so requires complex aural patterns and syllabic orderliness, is simply thrilling. I like to think I learnt a great deal from what I did then.

As for the Greek poets I've encountered, either in reading or through personal contact, I've said something about this in 92 *Acharnon Street*, the book I wrote about the year I spent as Lord Byron Visiting Professor at the University of Athens, where the glory was all in the title. But reading, and shaking hands with, poets who'd been under sentence of death (Anagnostakis, Ritsos – or Denegris, who lived for years in exile) invites at best a quizzical response to Anthony Hecht's claim that being an American poet demands a terrible sacrifice. I'm proud that Shoestring has published versions of several Greek writers, from Solomos, the 'National poet', to my good friend and joyous, Aristophanic spirit Katerina Anghelaki-Rooke, now sadly dead.

I could go on.

The press has quite a small web presence, which rather bucks the trend.

Yes, comparatively small. I used to be represented by a company who as good as told me that without their expert help I'd never get anywhere. But I do. Most of my titles sell pretty well – thanks in part to my excellent distributors, Central Books, and our book typesetters. I should also mention my printers, Imprint Digital, who can turn print runs round faster than I can think of terms of abuse for the Arts Council, from which I've long ceased to solicit a grant, even the very small one which was all I ever had. There was a period when the Council adopted as motto 'thrive not survive'. As far as I could discover, this meant that if you had published ten books in the previous year, this year you should aim to publish twenty. I asked the man from Yorkshire Arts, who was 'heading up' this ambitious project, whether he might like to double the number of Shoestring titles he had perhaps previously bought. He said he didn't buy books.

Is that the only reason you've not applied more recently for funding from Arts Council England? Your distaste for ACE is evident, but what do you think it gets wrong?

Over the years I grew increasingly appalled by the waste of money on what seemed to me vanity projects and on the stupidities of misapplied bureaucracy. Jobs for the boys and girls. Some twenty years ago they wanted to visit me to ensure that I was an Equal Opportunities employer, and that my work premises had 'suitable access' for disabled employees. I pointed out what they anyway knew: that I alone ran Shoestring Press from an upstairs room in my own house. Nevertheless, a visit was putatively arranged and a day set aside during which three (I think it was) ACE representatives would interview me and inspect my 'premises'. At which point I withdrew my then current grant application. Prior to this what I suspect must have been a vast sum went on moving the regional ACE premises from a perfectly suitable building in Loughborough to swankydom on Nottingham's Castle Gate. The extensive premises here were kitted out with various studios, and access was through a sort of secretarial office which would have been thought over the top for some London/International Bank. Again, I could go on...

Probably best we leave that there! Has editing books for Shoestring had much of an influence on your own poetry, do you think?

I try to keep my own writing as a thing apart. Now that I write mostly prose fiction I'm aware of certain influences on me, but they come from long ago and/or far away.

What are some of them? And why nothing contemporary and closer to home?

Arnold Bennett: *Anna of the Five Towns*, *Clayhanger*, a masterpiece, and *The Pretty Lady*, set in London during the First World War, a novel nobody seems to have read but which explains why T.S. Eliot was so keen to consult Bennett when he himself was at work on 'Sweeney Agonistes'. Peter Lovesey, a crime novelist wonderfully good

at registering the environment and atmosphere of events and whose characters are rarely taken from Central Casting; and anything by Robert Edric, one of the best novelists now at work. The recent *Mercury Falling*, set in a kind of off-limits East Anglia, and published like most of Edric's twenty plus novels by TransWorld, is superb, as good if not better than even Graham Swift's *Waterlands*. More recent is *My Own Worst Enemy*, Edric's memoir about growing up in working-class Sheffield, which Shoestring published last year. (It's now been reissued by a trade publisher, and quite right too.) Poets: from long ago, as it were, Thomas Hardy and Edwin Arlington Robinson ('Mr Flood's Party'), then Louis Simpson (the poems that came out of his experiences in wartime France, plus 'My Father in the Night Commanding No' and 'Walt Whitman at Bear Mountain'), then Peter Porter, Anne Stevenson, Matt Simpson, all now dead, and, still very much alive, Deryn Rees-Jones, and, a more recent discovery, Kate Bingham, whose *Infragreen* (2015) is a joy. I can't end without mentioning Maurice Rutherford, born in working-class Hull in 1922, and without doubt the most naturally gifted poet I know, a true original. *Nascitur non fecit*. All praise to Harry Chambers of Peterloo Poets, who published two of Maurice's collections, before, in 1997, Shoestring brought out his new and selected, *And Saturday is Christmas*.

One of the disadvantages of being my age (eighty-five) is that it's all too easy to under/overestimate younger writers. I think of Yeats reprimanding his juniors: 'Irish poets, learn your trade, / Sing whatever is well made. / Scorn the kind now growing up / All out of shape from toe to top.' Who could he have in mind? MacNeice, perhaps? Blimey. And in 1833, Coleridge found the young Tennyson 'metrically licentious'. *I'll* never make such mistakes, oh no. But still. That's why I'm hesitant about passing judgement on those you call contemporary and closer to home.

Nascitur non fecit – not a phrase likely to be adopted as the motto for a Creative Writing course...

No, though even great poets benefit from advice.

You've written about a book a year since the late 1960s: poetry, criticism, novels, memoirs, biographies, edited volumes. Your subjects have ranged from whistling to the Second World War, from George Crabbe to cricket. How on earth have you found the time and mental energy?

No idea, but I enjoy the act of writing. I admire Hazlitt's range as essayist: from meetings with poets to attending prize fights. American writers are better at covering such a range, aren't they? Though nobody compares with Dickens.

One of the first books you edited, when you were in your twenties, was your selection from Crabbe. What drew you to him then, and to what extent does that influence endure?

An essay by Forster in *Two Cheers for Democracy* fired the gun. Then I came across a sonnet by Edwin Arlington Robinson, praising Crabbe's 'hard, human pulse', and at about the same time I found that although Wordsworth sneered at Crabbe's matter-of-factness, Byron was an admirer – 'Nature's sternest painter and her best' – and Jane Austen claimed she wanted to be 'the second Mrs Crabbe'. I read him and at once enlisted for the cause. No wonder most of the important nineteenth-century novelists so admired him. He's a master of dialogue, of psychological narrative, and nobody does the atmosphere of landscape better than him. And, a clincher, when he went on walks around his Trowbridge parish, he and his son took with them bat, ball and stumps.

Coming from outside the kind of cultural orthodoxy still dominant in the 1950s and 1960s prompted me to champion writers who weren't part of the 'great tradition'. Hence my joy in discovering as well as Crabbe, Clare, and above all, Dickens. Leavis instructed his epigoni that Dickens had no higher purpose than 'entertainment'. So 'Right, you buggers', to quote Tony Harrison.

In your introduction to A Selection from George Crabbe, *you made quite a point of his isolated origins: 'there were no swift means of transport to the main cities, few reasons for going there, and still fewer for townspeople to go to the villages.' You grew up in rural Leicestershire. Is that the kinship you mean, when you talk about 'coming from outside the cultural orthodoxy'?*

It has much more to do with class position than geography, though they're connected. Still, 'poshos' could get to London and so on when they wanted. Others couldn't, or didn't feel the need. If I had to identify my parents in terms of class, I'd say they were lower middle, and I'd also say that a litmus test for being in that class is the ease, or otherwise, you'd feel about going into a modern art gallery. The first time I went into one I was seventeen, feeling pretty defiant, though six years earlier I'd accompanied a 'posher' part of the family into a gallery in St Ives. I can still remember something of the prickle of unease I felt. 'Not for the likes of us.' Crabbe must have felt like that. His father was a clever man, but he wasn't educated to the level that would've made it possible to be part of 'society', and nor was his son. Fanny Burney, born near Kings Lynn, was desperate to get to London, to escape the restrictions of her birthplace. But she felt the restrictions because she was reasonably well educated.

Especially in your collection Things to Say *(2010), there are many allusions to Philip Larkin, often argued with or undermined: 'If what will survive of us is love, / what will survive of those who lack for it', for instance. Or the closing couplet of 'Thorn Gruin's Sorrowful Sonnet': 'Night comes on. Waves fold behind villages. / What better excuse to go out and get pissed.' What draws you enduringly to his phrases?*

Not long ago, Hugo Williams admitted wryly to me that when *New Lines* appeared in 1955, he put his money on John Wain as the coming poet. So did my friend Matt Simpson. They were by no means alone in this. I've been wrong about many things, but I've always been sure that Larkin is a major poet. I know the flaws: 'surprising/wise in' (what might be called the Priti Patel school of rhyme), the misuse of idiom ('plugging at'), indulgence in bathetic endings ('the only end of age') and the racism, misogyny, etc, though these charges are overdone. The ending of 'For Sidney Bechet', a poem I love, is, I admit, a bit wonky: 'Long-haired grief and scored pity'. It's a brilliant double pun; in the 1950s classical musicians were called 'long hairs' and then there's Niobe, while 'scored' refers to non-improvised music as well as trenched lines on a grieving face. (But as Michael Longley asked, 'What's wrong with Mozart?') Peccadilloes, though, when weighed in balance. Do you know the story about Lowell and Randall Jarrell meeting to discuss English post-war poets? Which three did Lowell rate highest, Jarrell asked. Larkin, Gunn and Hughes, Lowell said. And Jarrell? Larkin, Larkin and Larkin.

I suspect your answer wouldn't be 'Larkin, Larkin, Larkin'. You haven't made much of a case for him.

He is an inescapable presence, and some at least of his poems are unforgettable. Alvarez's attempt to claim the superiority of Ted Hughes's 'Horses' over 'At Grass' is plain silly. Years ago I said in the intro to *Starting to Explain*, a collection of my essays on twentieth-century poetry, that in 1954 poetry entered my world. The following year, when I read Larkin in *New Lines*, I found that my world had entered poetry. I don't know any other poet of post-war England who uses so much of topography, of views of town and country, in order to let you know where you are, nor any other poet with such flexible control of the iambic.

What are your future plans for Shoestring, and for yourself?

If I manage to stay alive for a few more years, Shoestring can celebrate its thirtieth anniversary. That will do. I have a new short novel with my publishers and when I finished it I struck the board and cried 'No more'. But now I find myself writing about various people, 'mere, uncounted folk', who at different times of my life have meant much to me.

Four Poems

CLAUDINE TOUTOUNGI

Aftermath

If you were here we might discuss it all

> the rhyme-schemes of starlings
> the ramifications of squirrels
> that creature, that hyena laughing
> in the trees and how the blue hour
> really feels and why it is that song
> thrush always likes to smash
> an escargot into the wall

Detour to Rapture

Strange to come upon them shoving and rubbing
shoulders (without shoulders), charging about

a sure-fire shoal, a mass of marmalade bodies
in perpetual, Brownian motion. Why should I feel

so buoyed up by them? Or that I did right to spurn
the Cast Iron plant, skirt the Yucca and glancing

down – spy them? I have seen the signs. I have
heard the spheres dancing. O celestial slipstream!

O quixotic drift of all that is dart and dazzle. I have lost
my mind! I have left it in a fountain in Birmingham.

Misstep

I always like a bare-branched tree in winter.
The branches remind me of my dendrites.
Likewise a swoop of unidentified dive-
bombers can be companionable when there's
frost to crunch and elsewhere only the odd,
demented cackle from a fly-by, loner crow.
And my shadow's out in front, like I've a friend
leading the way. *Je suis* à *la file indienne
avec mon ombre,* you might say, if you were
trying to impress an intellectual, the sort who
later, over speciality hummus, might delicately
bring up your choice of old world diction and
raise an eyebrow at it, musing on locutions
that, really, didn't ought to be.

The Party

In the midst of life I told my host (who was in the kitchen) I needed
to slip out and stagger about in the yard for a bit and potentially
regurgitate into a woodpile the nibbles I'd hoovered up after a 4 hr
jamming session, during which I'd played bongos beatifically then
got locked in the toilet for hours because everyone else was busy
making jazz hands and scatting and they thought the screaming
was part of the music and the music worked well with my screams.

Three Poems

MAITREYABANDHU

LGBT, an Abridged History

Squirming under a towel on Sennen beach,
I watch my brothers, already daredevil
and beefy, run headlong into the sea
while my father reads *The Godfather*
on the Rover's hot front seat and my sister,
still in her water-wings, taps the glass
and passes him a paper cup of tea.
The scene is set for the household comedy
of growing up. My father's Burma letters
pressed away with Bristol Beaufighters
and Urdu in indecipherable script spell out
the ravages of the war but now I'm back
from art college again with Alison Moyet
on cassette. He'd read a letter I left out
that spoke of Gary not as friend but lover
and thinking it a blip (as if to prove
the truth of the Freudian slip) called him
'Larry' from then on – soon enough
I'd be over it and not be, as he feared,
lonely in my old age. So how to tell
his ghost (spending forever in the shed)
about the girls, their different mums, Alex
saying 'Maitreyabandhu's not a daddy,
he's just a *person*', Ria's diet of breadsticks;
girls to feed and get to bed in a sea-lit
rented bach with someone else's books –
An Angel at My Table, *War and Peace* –
arrested on a shelf; that from poring over
Muscle Magazine sequestered in the bathroom
to a love I'd thought beyond me is but the pull –
'Hold my hand, darling' – of history.

The Fallacy of Misplaced Concreteness

i.m Urygen Sangharakshita

By next morning spring was pushing back
the clouds, deepening the creases where
the farms were tucked away while the goddess,
risen above your bed in white appliqué,
offered her protection. (What *was* she playing at?)
Like discontented winter next to spring,
your cardigans, grey as post-war Britain,
droop beside your gold Tibetan shirt.
I found it beside your bed, the ceramic head
that Terry gave you, handsome butcher's son –
friendship's clear light of day stitched
like Dante's stars in heaven's blanket during
long talks late at night. Two policemen
turned up at your flat with your address
tucked inside his pocket. He'd bought a ticket
for the Underground at Kentish Town
then threw himself under – the scream he'd cut
in clay fixed forever. Time's passageway
reverberates with the voice of George V
'I thought men like that shot themselves'
as Leonardo's Lady, ermine twisting
on her arm, gazes through the window
(which window shall I choose: round or square?)
to where a lacquered bonnet, dotted white
with freshly fallen snow, floats across
the view as Master Bashō, staff in hand,
sets off for (or is coming back from?)
Irago. Forgive this. Forgive my foolishness.
Bless me as you once did, 'now and always'.
For March light is entering your room
and April light and May light, and soon the summer
weather will kindle Pseudo-Dionysius,
Thom Gunn, *The Life of Proclus*. The ducks have flown
(walked more like!) between two muddy ponds.
I wish that I could shake your hand, call you
by our intimate, by our everyday address.

Snow on Hampstead, 2018

My iPhone tells me frostily: snow,
100% chance of snow at 11am
and already the sky's dishcloth-whiteness is heavy
with old silverware, Habsburg crystal,
my mother's mother-of-pearl, as first flakes rise
in flurries to fall on children's playground, church
and sports hall, while The Ghost of Christmas Past
retreats into its future, tail-lights red.
The girls are working at being underwhelmed
though even Alex permits a 'cringy' selfie
and a hug as the trampled snowmen
we walk through – ghoul-faced or laurel-crowned –
recapitulate, in broken arms and heads,
the life of Father Time. 'Someone's made
an angel and a swan!' I call to tell them
but they're way ahead talking in a language
only teenagers understand beyond the last word
of this poem where girlhood is translated
into the killing of George Floyd, riot police
on Capitol Hill, Oxford-AstraZeneca.
That was still their future. Just for now
they've grown beyond the roundabout and seesaw
two-inches taller for the snow while our love,
our little love – Gary's, mine – might be
a rope tied round their waists as they linger, talking.

From the Archive

from *PNR* 170, Volume 32 Number 6, 2006

To C.G.

I thought I saw you on the bus today;
started to smile, then quickly turned away
before he saw (of course, he wasn't you)
I'd dressed him by mistake in borrowed robes.
I didn't look again, but couldn't shake
the sense that you'd just reappeared. As though
you'd moved away – taken a job down south,
maybe, or gone abroad, brushed up your languages –
and just got back. As though you might pop round
later this week, and we'd pick up where we
left off, nine years ago next month. As though
you'd had a nice safe job, not been a priest,
not tried to help that man that night. As though
he hadn't had a knife, and you weren't dead.

HELEN TOOKEY

Three Poems

NICOLA HEALEY

Death of a Field Mouse

At the edge of my eye
the size of a bird's head
fell off the pavement

like a drunk. Dazed,
he let me watch him.
He stumbled, legs splayed,

but then eyes narrowed
like a cat's in the sun.
He turned one way,

then another, then tried
just being still
with a heartbeat

wider than his body.
He leapt towards me –
stopped. Circled himself

like he was becoming
clockwork, and someone
had turned a key.

He huddled by a primrose
and then the watering can,
and then I left him.

I can't find the clinical
kindness to kill a life
in need of release.

I found his finished body
in the morning
under the bay tree,

wreathed in laurel leaves.
This death is not
on me, yet it's on me.

The Unsaid

I polished writing like tidying hair:
to be considerate, received.

A clear sentence wears assurance
like an insect in amber.
We find that gem beautiful,
forgetting the struggle it conceals.

It oozed from a tree like blood
to seal a wound. A fly, stuck, starved
or drowned as its spiracles
filled with sticky resin.

The living inclusion preserved
in paralysis.

So it seems, writing is both
true and false;
a saviour and a traitor.

How easily we are deceived,
how narrow are even great minds.

To see through the words
is where we meet
in the hum of wisdom.

Philadelphus 'Belle Étoile'

(Mock Orange) I

Buds in June: curls of clotted cream.
Flowers white with hidden purple streams,

like the capillaries in your wrist. Scent:
the clarity of orange blossom, fresh and sweet,

simply my spirit.

All the summers it dispensed to the air.
That year, I noticed each starry flower

breathed their breath

noticed them as they fell.
And when the last withered petal fell,

knowing it would bloom again in a year
alone was enough to keep me here.

'A Cabbage in the Rain'

D.H. Lawrence's *Birds, Beasts and Flowers* at 100

ROWLAND BAGNALL

When they are considered at all, the poems of D.H. Lawrence tend to be praised for their engagements with the natural world. Lawrence's 'great gift', writes Marjorie Perloff, was his 'Wordsworthian ability "to see into the life of things,"' lifting a phrase from 'Tintern Abbey'. 'He seemed able to enter into other lives, and not only human lives', recalled Jessie Chambers, with whom Lawrence had his first significant relationship: 'With wild things, flowers and birds, a rabbit in a snare, the speckled eggs in a hole in the ground he was in primal sympathy – a living vibration passed between him and them, so that I always saw him, in the strictest sense of the word, immortal.' In her memoir *Not I, but the Wind* (1936), Frieda Weekley – Lawrence's wife, widow, and sparring partner – paints a similar portrait of her husband the naturalist. 'When [he] first found a gentian', she notes, recounting an episode from their alpine honeymoon in 1912, 'I remember feeling as if he had a strange communion with it, as if the gentian yielded up its blueness, its very essence, to him.'

Even before the publication of *Birds, Beasts and Flowers* – which celebrates its centenary in 2023 – Lawrence's poetry is frequently grounded in enigmatic run-ins with the natural world. 'A Doe at Evening', from *Look! We Have Come Through!* (1917), dramatizes an encounter with a single, silhouetted deer, 'a fine black blotch / on the sky'. The poem speaks directly to Lawrence's 'great gift' for seeing beyond the veneer of outward appearances:

I looked at her
and felt her watching;
I became a strange being.
Still, I had my right to be there with her.
Her nimble shadow trotting
along the sky-line, she
put back her fine, level-balanced head.
And I knew her.

Lawrence finds himself under an equal scrutiny, gazed at – even *into* – by the deer, a disarming experience that transforms him into 'a strange being,' somehow exposed, unbalanced like the uneven metrical arrangements of each quatrain, whose lines can't seem to make their minds up about which pattern of feet to take. But the experience also permits Lawrence to claim new knowledge of the deer, albeit with the acceptance, in the poem's final stanza, of his own animal nature:

Ah yes, being male, is not my head hard-balanced, antlered?
Are not my haunches light?
Has she not fled on the same wind as me?
Does not my fear cover her fear?

The questions here are doubtful, unsure of themselves, but they suggest – 'Ah yes' – both revelation and discovery. More importantly, they speak to an equalization of some kind, the poet and the deer sharing not only the same evening but 'the same wind' and even something of the same anatomy, 'level-balanced' against each other.

'A Doe at Evening' interrogates the natural world, staring long and hard at it, meeting its gaze. But it also seems to hinge upon the difference between looking and knowing, observing and understanding, or – to use the language of the poem's second stanza – between 'watching' and 'being'. Rather than entering into another life, as Jessie Chambers has it, this poem seems to finish on a note of flat uncertainty, as if the revelation that was promised had suddenly 'fled'. A case of *Almost, but not quite.*

Many readers have found the natural world to be somehow deciphered in Lawrence's poems, its 'very essence' laid bare, to echo Frieda Weekley. Time and again, however, we encounter a blockage, a failure to discover any kinship with the world at all. As Lawrence suggests of a group of autumn cyclamens, recalling a trip to Lake Garda in 1913, his writing is filled with 'little living myths that [he] cannot understand.' Far from seeing into the life of things, more often than not we find their essences eluding him.

*

The poems in *Birds, Beasts and Flowers* are frequently considered to be the peak of Lawrence's poetic achievement. Written between 1920 and 1923, they span one of the poet's most restless periods of international travel. Beginning in San Gervasio, outside Florence, the poems head south to Sicily before migrating back to Austria and Spain; returning to Italy, they set sail for Sri Lanka, then Australia, and arrive, at long last, in New Mexico, where the voyage of the collection ends. The book is divided into several sections, grouping the poems into a system of ecological classification, from 'Fruits', 'Trees', and 'Flowers' to 'Reptiles', 'Birds', and 'Animals'. With a handful of exceptions, the poems consider natural subjects, offering a deep investigation into ideas of otherness and symbolism.

The collection has proven popular. Lawrence himself considered it to be his 'best book of poems', and many have gone on to become among his most anthologised pieces of writing. Among their admirers is Joyce Carol Oates, who conducts a radical defence of Lawrence's poetry in her book *The Hostile Sun* (1973). Oates interprets Lawrence's writing, in part, as a reaction to the Romantic view of Nature as a means of symbolic or spiritual access to divinity. For Oates, the poems are resolutely anti-spiritual. Lawrence 'is not trying to project himself into these creatures', she writes, 'nor is he really trying to interpret them. They remain alien, brute, [and] essentially unknowable.'

The poems quickly introduce us to Lawrence's persistent language of inquiry, a precise and at times almost casual mode of questioning, as in the following lines from 'Bare Almond-Trees':

> What are you doing in the December rain?
> Have you a strange electric sensitiveness in your
>   steel tips?
> Do you feel the air for electric influences
> Like some strange magnetic apparatus?
> Do you take in messages, in some strange code,
> From heaven's wolfish, wandering electricity, that
> prowls so constantly round Etna?
> Do you take the whisper of sulphur from the air?
> Do you hear the chemical accents of the sun?
> Do you telephone the roar of the waters over the
>   earth?
> And from all this, do you make calculations?

'Like iron implements twisted, hideous, out of the earth', as he describes them in the opening stanza, Lawrence's almond trees don't, won't, or can't answer him. Their silence is solidified by Lawrence's strange metallicizing process, turning them first to iron and then to 'sensitive steel'. Their branches become 'steel tips', feeling out 'Like some strange magnetic apparatus' (resembling a lightning rod), straining for 'messages, in some strange code', receiving and transmitting like a 'telephone'. The trees possess a set of meanings Lawrence has no way to understand; the mechanical and electrical (not to mention *metrical*) tools at his disposal are simply not up to the task. As Keith Sagar writes of 'Cypresses', another poem in the collection, 'If the trees are messengers, [then] their message is undecipherable, cannot be rendered into discursive language.'

We come away from *Birds, Beasts and Flowers* compelled by the resistance of Lawrence's subjects to be pinned down by the poems. As he puts it at the end of one of the collection's best-known pieces: 'But I, I only wonder / And don't know. / I don't know fishes.' By tracing the movement of signifiers and signifieds, Amit Chaudhuri has illustrated the sheer refusal of Lawrence's language to mean (and *only* mean) one thing,

revealing how the imagery of one poem may inform and/or revise another. For Joyce Carol Oates, the collection amounts to a kind of 'worship', whereby Lawrence ultimately embraces his inability to understand the natural world's 'strange code[s]'. To go one step further, it's as if Lawrence wants to find a way to let the natural world speak for itself, a quality he champions in the painter Paul Cézanne: 'Cézanne's apples are a real attempt to let the apple exist in its own separate entity, without transfusing it with personal emotion', he writes in the introduction to a book of his own paintings, suggesting that Cézanne's 'great effort' was 'to shove the apple away from him, and let it live of itself'.

*

Birds, Beasts and Flowers was completed in New Mexico in February 1923. While Lawrence had long desired to visit the United States – he wrote to many friends expressing his idea to establish an artistic colony in Florida and had been working sporadically on a survey of eighteenth- and nineteenth-century American writing, later published as *Studies in Classic American Literature* (1923) – he and Frieda, arriving into San Francisco on a ship bound from New Zealand, would not reach America until September 1922, a week shy of Lawrence's thirty-seventh birthday.

Lawrence had been invited to New Mexico by Mabel Dodge Luhan, a New York writer and self-styled patron of the avant-garde who contacted him on the strength of an extract of *Sea and Sardinia* (1921), and urged him to come and tackle the American Southwest. He had been critical of Europe's direction following the First World War, and America had been on his mind as the obvious site of the century's future. Rejecting the tired, monotheistic and increasingly mechanised world of the European continent, a canvas of crumbling monuments, Lawrence discovered inspiration in America's indigenous communities. Here, he found an alternative tradition, older than the ancient Greeks, which seemed to value, above all, a profound spiritual connection between the human and the natural worlds. 'How marvellous is the living relationship between man and his object!' he wrote in 1925, 'be it man or woman, bird, beast, flower or rock or rain; the exquisite frail moment of pure conjunction, which, in the fourth dimension, is timeless.'

Lawrence returns to this idea, to the 'exquisite frail moment of pure conjunction', many times throughout his writing. Very often, he reaches for the word 'contact' to articulate his thinking. In an essay on New Mexico, published posthumously in 1931, he describes the attempt of Native American religious rituals to 'come into immediate *felt* contact' with 'the elemental life of the cosmos, mountain-life, cloud-life, thunder-life, air-life, earth-life, sun-life' and so on, a 'sheer naked contact, *without an intermediary or mediator*' (recalling his comments on Cézanne). 'Oh when man has escaped from the barbed-wire entanglement / of his own ideas and his own mechanical devices' reads his poem 'Terra Incognita', 'there is a marvellous rich world of contact and sheer fluid beauty', a 'fearless face-to-face awareness'.

'Contact' is a word implying intimacy, exposure, and the physicality of touch. For Lawrence, it carried the spirit of the American frontier, conjuring images of pioneers making contact with indigenous communities. He may also have been channelling a passage from Thoreau, who, descending Maine's Mount Katahdin, finds himself in a truly wild, untamed environment, which triggered a moment of ecstasy: 'Talk of mysteries! – Think of our life in nature, – daily to be shown matter, to come in contact with it, – rocks, trees, wind on our cheeks! The solid earth! the *actual* world! the *common sense! Contact! Contact! Who* are we? *where* are we?'

Most importantly of all, 'contact' is a word that Lawrence would have recognised from Whitman, 'the great poet, who has meant so much to me', as he puts it (with surprising sincerity) in *Studies in Classic American Literature*.

*

Lawrence's relationship with Whitman's writing (and homosexuality) was far from straightforward: there are several early versions of the 'Whitman' essay in *Studies*, ranging from the enthusiastically praiseworthy to the wildly critical and frequently crass; Lawrence gives Whitman 'the roughest ride ever accorded him', according to poet Robert Creeley. At the same time, the influence of Whitman's poetry is clear on works like 'New Heaven and Earth', from *Look! We Have Come Through!*, 'in some respects the most profoundly Whitmanian poem not written by Walt' for Harold Bloom. The final poem in *Birds, Beasts and Flowers*, 'The American Eagle', interrupts its meditation with a series of onomatopoeic interjections mimicking the eagle's cry, complete with a loud, capitalised 'YAWP!!!' plucked straight from the pages of 'Song of Myself'.

The word 'contact' appears six times in the 1855 edition of *Leaves of Grass*. 'I will go to the bank by the wood and become undisguised and naked' writes Whitman in the book's opening stanzas, 'I am mad for it to be in contact with me', lines rehearsed by Lawrence in a scene from *Women in Love* (1920) in which Birkin, lying on a hillside, surrounded by flowers, decides to take off all his clothes:

> He wanted to touch them all, to saturate himself with the touch of them all. He took off his clothes, and sat down naked among the primroses [...] It was such a fine, cool, subtle touch all over him, he seemed to saturate himself with their contact.

Whitman's 'contact' is a physical encounter between separate bodies, between one thing and another. It seems likely that the word is borrowed from the language of photography, referring to a method of darkroom development in which a negative is placed directly onto photographic paper (known as a *contact sheet*) before being exposed to light. As Whitman critic Ed Folsom has noted, it's important to remember that Whitman's poetry 'emerged at precisely the time photography was literally taking hold of the American imagination', teaching the poet 'to see how all the actual stuff of the world was crucial to its wholeness'. In *The Dyer's Hand* (1963), Auden acknowledges the photographic quality of Whitman's poetry – somewhat fittingly – in his essay about D.H. Lawrence, noting how 'No detail is dwelt upon for long' but rather 'snapshotted and added as one more item to the vast American catalogue'.

Folsom convincingly argues how Whitman anticipates the 'intense, fragmentary, momentary seeing' of Ezra Pound's Imagism, with which Lawrence was peripherally associated (appearing in Amy Lowell's anthology *Some Imagist Poets* in 1915). For Lawrence, it is the photographic, spontaneous Whitman – the poet of contact, not democracy – who gets closest to understanding 'the pure frail moment of pure conjunction', the same 'living relationship between man and his object' he describes in 1925. In *Studies*, this is a quality he recognises as Whitman's great philosophy of 'The Open Road', and praises the poet's receptiveness (even vulnerability) to the world on its own terms, 'Exposed to full contact. On two slow feet. Meeting whatever comes.'

*

Lawrence's own poetry has been criticised for its excessive spontaneity. In 1935, the American critic R.P. Blackmur advanced an attack on his writing, citing its apparent lack of technical ability as an extreme version of the contemporary 'plague of expressive form'. A decade later, lecturing on Whitman to the Churchill Club, T.S. Eliot suggested that Lawrence's poems 'are more notes for poems than poems themselves', while Keith Sagar described the work in Lawrence's collection *Pansies* (1929) as not much more 'than notebook jottings', concluding that the worst 'do not even have the virtues of good prose'.

It's easy enough to find examples of Lawrence's poetry that confirm the worst of these criticisms – try the posthumous *More Pansies* (1932) – but it seems important to measure Lawrence's attempts at spontaneity not only in the context of his thinking about Whitman but in his desire to achieve in writing what Cézanne had done in paint, to discover the 'immediate *felt* contact' between himself and his experience.

A short essay of 1919, 'Poetry and the Present' is the closest thing to a poetic manifesto Lawrence ever came to writing. Originally published as a preface to the American edition of *New Poems* (1920), Lawrence used the essay as an opportunity to advocate for a new type of poetics. He begins by distinguishing between two presiding movements, one a poetry of the past, the other of the future, both striving for 'perfected moments' of thought and experience, encapsulated, he suggests, by 'the treasured gem-like lyrics of Shelley and Keats'. 'But there is another kind of poetry', he continues, 'the poetry of that which is at hand: the immediate present.' Rather than create the 'everlasting gems' of past or future experience, Lawrence's proposal is to somehow apprehend the energy and spontaneity of the present moment before it crystalizes into something else, to create a 'seething poetry of the incarnate Now'. In 'the immediate present', reads a striking passage, nothing is fixed:

> there is no perfection, no consummation, nothing fin-

ished. The strands are flying, quivering, intermingling into the web, the waters are shaking the moon. There is no round, consummate moon on the face of running water, nor on the face of the unfinished tide. There are no gems of the living plasm. The living plasm vibrates unspeakably, it inhales the future, it exhales the past, it is the quick of both, and yet it is neither. There is no plasmic finality, nothing crystal, permanent.

This passage is typical of the essay. Lawrence offers up an 'intermingling [...] web' of natural images, from the turbulent running waters, distorting their surface-image of the moon, to the gentle inhaling and exhaling of time and the mysterious 'living plasm', an image he returns to often. The repetitious nature of Lawrence's writing gives an impression of him scribbling down his thoughts as they occur, as if trying to capture them before they disappear, building on images and ideas as he goes, sentence by sentence, maintaining a relentless forward momentum that enacts the very lack of fixity he's eager to describe, the essay rushing by in glimpses, a river of present tense participles: 'flying', 'quivering', 'shaking', 'living'.

This is a quality of Lawrence's writing acknowledged by several readers. In *Out of Sheer Rage* (1997), Geoff Dyer suggests that 'everything is written – rather than noted and then written – as experienced' in Lawrence, identifying an immediacy in which 'The transformation from "notes" to "prose" often takes place within the course of a sentence'. 'It was characteristic of him that he hardly ever corrected or patched what he had written', recalls Aldous Huxley in his introduction to an edition of Lawrence's *Selected Letters*: 'If he was dissatisfied with what he had written, he did not, as most authors do, file, clip, insert, transpose; he re-wrote.'

The 'poetry of the incarnate Now' is necessary to Lawrence, I think, as a way of trying to make contact with the world of things head-on. Because life and experience exist in constant 'flux' (another favourite word of his), it seems obvious that poetry should at least try to reflect this, to emulate 'the quality of life itself', as Lawrence puts it in the essay. Not only might this enable the poem to partake in 'the very white quick of nascent creation', but, crucially, the attempt offers the poet themselves an opportunity to participate in 'the very substance of creative change'. It is in this moment of creative mutation – the continuous coming-into-being of the present moment – that the potential for 'immediate *felt* contact' between the poet and the world is most acutely possible.

Perhaps unsurprisingly, it is Whitman's poetry that Lawrence sees as coming closest to achieving this. 'Without beginning and without end, without any base and pediment', he writes, 'it sweeps past for ever, like a wind that is for ever in passage.' 'There was never any more inception than there is now, / Nor any more youth or age than there is now, / And will never be any more perfection than there is now, / Nor any more heaven or hell than there is now', writes Whitman in 'Song of Myself', a sequence whose line-endings appear to channel Lawrence's poetics of immediacy: *there is now, there is now, there is now, there is now*.

Very often, Lawrence's poetry reveals his own pursuit of this immediacy. 'Hostile critics have called [them] "sketches for poems"', acknowledges Keith Sagar, 'but a sketch is often superior, in terms of life, to the finished product.' As Frieda wrote of Lawrence, 'Everything he met had the newness of a creation that had just that moment come into being', a 'newness' – or a *now*-ness – that he transmitted to his writing. At their best, his poems retain the unpredictable, even chaotic spirit of this creation, preserved in such a way that future readers might be able to experience the same, as if the energy of Lawrence's 'sheer present' were still radiating from the text itself. As he wrote of his collection *Pansies*, Lawrence saw his poems as 'merely the breath of the moment, and one eternal moment easily contradicting the next eternal moment', exposing – in his paradoxical 'eternal moment' – a delicate hairline fracture between the 'contact' of the present and the borders of eternity. I'm reminded, again, of Jessie Chambers: 'a living vibration passed between him' and the natural world, 'so that I always saw him, in the strictest sense of the word, immortal.'

Lawrence died in France, aged forty-four, in March of 1930. Whether his poetry amounts to an expression of the 'incarnate Now' or not, there is a strange prophetic quality to his ideas about the direction poetry is taking in the 1920s. At the very least, it seems a shame that he didn't live long enough to witness the emergence of a new generation of American poets explicitly devoted to the textures of the present tense. Like him, these poets would celebrate the speed and the stuff of 'the incarnate Now', relishing – as Geoff Dyer notes of Lawrence – 'the shock of the first encounter', and producing a body of poetry which, above all, ripples with 'immediate *felt* contact'.

In his foreword to *Parallel Movement of the Hands* (2022), a posthumous collection of John Ashbery's unpublished poems, Ben Lerner addresses the 'endlessly renewable' quality of Ashbery's writing. 'In a John Ashbery poem', he argues, 'we set the machinery of meaning-making into motion each time we read, each time we enter the poem's environment in the present tense.' The poems take place in a 'perpetual present', available to re-experience – as if for the first time – again and again and again and again.

The biography of the New York School poets – a cluster of mid-twentieth-century writers that includes Ashbery, Frank O'Hara, Kenneth Koch and Barbara Guest – is readily available, so I won't go into detail here (see Brad Gooch's *City Poet: The Life and Times of Frank O'Hara* (1993) and Karin Roffman's *The Songs We Know Best: John Ashbery's Early Life* (2017); for rolling, up-to-date New York School info, Andrew Epstein's *Locus Solus* blog posts are essential – newyorkschoolpoets.wordpress.com). While members of the so-called 'School' have expressed no desire in being taken as a group, they seem to share, at the very least, an interest in the possibilities of poetry's immediacy and *now*-ness.

Frank O'Hara's habit of dashing poems off during his lunch hour, in bars, at parties, even once *en route* to giving a reading (scribbling a new poem on the Staten Island Ferry), has become a marker of these poems' fizzingness and energy. 'The speed and accidental aspect of his writing are not carelessness but are essential to what the poems are about', wrote O'Hara's close friend, Kenneth Koch, 'the will to catch what is there while it is really there and still taking place.' This is a quality of O'Hara's poetry – a quality of constant coming and going, of life on the move – best put, perhaps, by Marjorie Perloff: 'Photographs, monuments, static memories […] have no place in the poet's world. We can now understand why O'Hara loves the *motion* picture, *action* painting, and all forms of dance – art forms that capture the *present* rather than the *past*, the present in all its moving, chaotic splendor.'

Likewise, Ashbery's poetry has been seen to reflect the textures of the present tense. While his poetry isn't so devoted as O'Hara's to capturing the material stuff of the world as it skids by, several readers (Lerner included) have commented on Ashbery's ability to mimic the real-time contours of experience and thought. 'Clepsydra', whose title refers to an ancient time-keeping device that uses water as its means of measurement, is 'really a meditation on how time feels as it is passing,' according to the poet; for the critic Stephen Ross, it reveals 'Ashbery's ambition to dissolve content into the pure flow of time'. Each line is 'scarcely called into being / Before it swells, the way a waterfall / Drums at different levels', to echo the poem, building an awareness of its liquid movement in 'Precisely the time of its being furthered'.

While these examples serve to illustrate a common thread tying the New York School together, there is one poet in particular who seems to answer Lawrence's call for a poetry of the present. Born in 1923, the year of Lawrence's *Birds, Beasts and Flowers*, James Schuyler fell in with New York's poets and painters in the early 1950s, following a stint in the US Navy and a spell abroad in Italy where he worked as Auden's secretary. Living for periods with both Ashbery and O'Hara, Schuyler worked at the Periscope-Holliday Bookstore, was a regular contributor to *ARTnews* (his *Selected Art Writings* was published in 1998), and became the curator for circulating exhibitions at the Museum of Modern Art. During the 1960s, long bouts of anxiety and mental illness saw him relocate to Southampton and Maine, where he was taken in by the painter Fairfield Porter and his family; as Porter's wife Anne once quipped, Schuyler 'came to lunch one day and stayed for eleven years'. Eventually, friends moved Schuyler into Room 625 of the Hotel Chelsea in Manhattan, where he lived for over a decade until his death in April 1991. Quiet, retiring and cripplingly shy, he gave his first public reading, aged sixty-five, at the DIA Foundation on Mercer Street, where he was lovingly introduced by Ashbery: 'I give you a poet who knows the names for things, and whose knowing proves something'.

*

The overriding tendency of Schuyler's poetry is a quality of dailiness. Fifteen of his *Collected Poems* (1993) include the date within their title, while a further thirty-three reference a season, month, or temporal marker. His most famous work is arguably 'The Morning of the Poem', a collage of gentle happenings and observations, unfolding in a running commentary, blending anecdotes, shopping lists and newspaper headlines with descriptions of the weather and the views or objects close-to-hand. 'The procedure of Schuyler's poems is to follow the divining rod of the moment in the direction in which it is being pulled', suggests Tom Clark in a review of the *Collected Poems*. As Schuyler writes himself of Fairfield Porter's paintings, '[their] art is one that values the everyday as the ultimate, the most varied and desirable knowledge'.

Schuyler's theme is change. More specifically, it is the strangeness of acknowledging both change and similarity. 'The / Days tick by, each so unique, each so alike', read lines towards the end of 'Hymn to Life', another famous long poem. 'Most things, like the sky', agrees 'Greenwich Avenue', 'are always changing, always the same.' Suspended between careful looking and attentiveness on the one hand and the casual, shrug-like nature of the incidental on the other, Schuyler's poetry, at heart, is a celebration of what is (simply put) *available*. 'What is, is by its nature, on display', he writes in an early poem. '[I want] merely to say, to see and say, things / as they are' suggests another, as if answering Wallace Stevens's question – 'So that's life, then: things as they are?' – with a low-key, half-bemused response: 'I guess so. What else would there be?'

What Schuyler achieves, I think, is something close to Lawrence's 'incarnate Now'. In contact with the immediate present – Lawrence's 'living plasm' – Schuyler's poems are truly of the moment, embracing both the *There* and *Then*. 'Now, this moment / flows out of me / down the pen and / writes', he suggests in 'Linen', collapsing the distance between 'moment' and 'poem', as if it was the same thing all along. In doing so, Schuyler not only manages to locate the frequency of the present, sensing the 'knowledge' in a vase of flowers, a glimpse through the window, the light hitting the tops of trees, but, at the same time, seems to understand (as Lawrence suggested of Cézanne) that the truest route to knowledge might be to let the world speak for itself, to observe it, to notice, but to allow for the possibility that 'Getting the most out of a stone might be to leave it alone', as he puts it in 'The Cenotaph'.

In this way, Schuyler's poems achieve a quality of livingness. Like Lawrence's 'eternal moment', they shudder like a handheld camera, like the hazy, endlessly rewindable footage of a home movie. Very often, reading Schuyler feels like reading something he has only just now finished working on, the ink not fully dry; like encountering a freshness of thought and observation that keeps the poems somehow alive and kicking. As Doug Crase puts it in his elegiac essay, 'The reality Jimmy wanted us always to have was a reality still alive.'

By celebrating life in flux, Schuyler, like Lawrence, pulls off the unexpected, stopping the moment in its tracks, a single, silhouetted deer, suspended in time like a scene in a snow globe. The poems allow us to revisit Schuyler's 'still alive' reality, to view the present alongside him, as if over his shoulder. They encapsulate what the late James Longenbach (1959–2022) has called the lyric poem's 'repeatable event of itself', recreating the moment 'as we enter it'; 'whether written in 1920 or 2020', the poem is always 'happening now.'

'Nothing is important but life', says Lawrence, 'And for myself, I can absolutely see life nowhere but in the living. Life with a capital L is only man alive. Even a cabbage in the rain is a cabbage alive.' 'It's the yellow dust inside the tulips', writes Schuyler in his poem 'February':

> It's the shape of a tulip.
> It's the water in the drinking glass the tulips are in.
> It's a day like any other.

Three Poems

D.W. BRYDON

Harbour

A carousel of little boats
up-downs to the music
of the huge moon
that is visiting this harbour.

The steeple of the kirk
spears the pink clouds
which dissolve into smirr
as the evening turns darker.

Inside the stone houses
the big wheel
is the only topic
on TV or radio.

Only astronomers
had cared at first
but now there is a face
at every window

and for the first time,
I can see it in the sky
growing rapidly larger
with each birl

and for the first time,
I can see how it swirls,
how it glisters
and feel ever more giddy,

I can sense how it tugs,
how it gyres, and feel
ever more buoyant, ever more flimsy
until I realise *it is me*

that is spinning, and keow
like the gulls, as I join them
and the radios and the TV sets
and the little boats and the stone houses
and the auld kirk and the whole world and the huge moon

Aftermath

Vermeil sky,
a half-aspirin of moon,
cumulus slowly spreads...

The morning world –
slates strewn pell-mell on the lawn.
The fence cants into the neighbour's garden.
A broken oak branch lies in dew
and in the mulberry tree, a bird sings
quietly, under a bloodshot sun.

Star-tank

I turn the dial:
a nebula glides past.

Its voice
is like a whale's.

A cerulean comet
eels around its orbital path.

Beyond Andromeda's spiral shell
interstellar corals sway.

Albireo pauses companionably:
golden clownfish and blue anemone.

At the conflux of two galaxies
the tentacles of Magellan grasp.

A fire urchin flares in the outer cosmos,
its spines spilling from a nuclear blast.

A seahorse head bursts
through Orion from the east.

Its startled cry
is a stellar wind.

I crank back the dial
four billion years:

A black hole suction-feeds
on the seabed of space-time.

Now I see a blastocyst
or is it a star nursery?

Now I see a ring galaxy
or is it a fish eye watching me?

Zooming in through space and time,
the same series of patterns repeats.

I zoom in further, further,
hoping for an asteroid hitting the sea

but instead I find myself
back in my childhood

listening to the different pitches
of the voices I create

as I play on the beach
with Russian dolls.

Three Poems

OLUWASEUN OLAYIWOLA

Beacon

Just secrets to the sea
is what we were, the moon

inside us, waxing,
as if astonishment, slipping
like oysters through

our throats, were
a type of force, the frozen
girdle of purple lips

struggling,
not to breathe, but with breath –

In the end, we made it
to the lighthouse, which was
never the point.

We climbed a ladder to the top
because there were no stairs

Night on the Thames Path

To have settled in the fraternal space between play and fight

To have, along the river, heard their names
        hovering in the head like an intellect of loss

To have bequeathed each name to a seabird posturing
        in the black water they sprung from: his name for the coot,

his for the moorhen, his, the cormorant, the mute
        swan at last lifting off its majesty as if the river

were not its birthplace, were not where it watched you run

unevenly, run as if the mind could be abandoned behind
        like ambition; to have existed, to have loved, to have been

in your existing, your loving, rare
        the way a bone deep in the rivered is still apart

of the assembling landscape as your foot steps far
        above on the shore in the sand into a beige never-thereness –

All my beloveds. Somehow, it is *like* they were never there –

Mausoleum

Two dogs sniff the garden for a friend; like any animals
for which mortality is simply a foliage pocked with holes,
a barrier, they don't know – no matter how putrescent
a loved body becomes – what they don't know. Is twelve
paw-prints (and I hope it's not) in their mind so different
from eight? They're in the proto-stage of grief's circle, where
the search is confirmation: until the body is found lifeless,
a bright light exists inside the nose like the north star: an illusion
that what you seek moves towards you as you seek it – See,
I wish there was language I could offer them, how you ruin
a game of cards because your face reveals your hand is good,
how gravitating to loss, the body collects sores like a mausoleum
that is never finished – Helplessness: what we're all mucking
around in, though the dogs possess no compass for probability –
I should have seen the dead body in the soil and called it *wonder*.
Now they're circling me with their faces dragging the earth
and I want to say *yield* – *yield* but neither of us knows how
aimless we are in this place smelling the future, how we are
hesitations time will not pause towards when it buries us –

'The civilising discourse'

An interview with Nyla Matuk

EVAN JONES

This interview was conducted via email between 18 June and 9 July 2022.

Nyla Matuk was born in Winnipeg, Manitoba, and raised in Ottawa, Ontario. She holds an MA in English from McGill University and is the author of two books of poetry: *Sumptuary Laws* (2012) and *Stranger* (2016). She is also the editor of an anthology of poems, *Resisting Canada* (2019). In 2018, she served as the Mordecai Richler Writer in Residence at McGill University. She works for the Department of Canadian Heritage arts sector and lives in Montreal.

*

EJ: Your poems have always been critical in their thinking – but beginning with the 2019 anthology you edited, Resisting Canada, there is a clearer political agenda. What were your motivations for putting the anthology together?

NM: It's fair to say the motivation for the anthology is rooted in my curiosity about the variability of poetry – how language might be both compelling and accountable outside matters tending to the personal; and how it might address the urgency of collective political consciousness with the consideration of social conditions. Or perhaps a consciousness of injustice. My political or justice awakening – a noticeable uptick in such consciousness – began in 2014, when for fifty-one days the world watched the merciless bombing of Palestinian refugees living in the region of historic Palestine known as Gaza, under blockade since 2006.

Seeing those fifty-one days via Twitter and other media left me physically numb and psychologically horrified. At the same time, more of the brutal history of residential schools in so-called Canada was being told – through the published memoirs of elders, Indigenous journalism and academic studies. The reckoning of settler-colonialism in at least two of its iterations – Canada and Israel – was all around us, then, and has continued to make itself known.

My own poetry stood in stark contrast to the resistance poems I started to read to prepare *Resisting Canada*. What emerged for me, and what I continue to think about as I have turned to writing fiction, is the irreconcilable tension between private experience and collective consciousness. Matters of collective knowledge I focused on were Palestine's ongoing anticolonial national liberation movement and the history of Indigenous Peoples closer to where I grew up. Coming of age in a settler-colony in the 70s and 80s, I perceived literary culture as fixated on works that take the individual romantic subject as the point of view, and often as subject matter. The anthology offered an alternative.

Most of the contemporary poetry I had been reading worked in that individuated register, not particularly aware of systemic oppression. Perhaps the latter makes too much purpose out of poetry and is therefore deservedly overlooked, or maybe we have not moved out of a need to find common cause with personal matters, another individual's hardships, joy, or existential crisis; the desire to discover a kindred spirit or friend at the end of a collection of poems?

I wanted to know how language – and poems in particular – could express something other than the travails and temperaments of the Kierkegaardian Individual, the lone figure of the *bildungsroman*, and so forth. I'm not sure that any of the poems I included fit the bill, but certainly this discrepancy was on top of my mind.

Can you say more about the notion of 'common cause'?

I meant that readers may seek a dyadic relationship with the poet; to find common cause in personal anguish, grief, or wonder and laughter (maybe that sounds a bit too much like 'Live! Love! Laugh!'). 'Common cause' may be the wrong description here... empathic consciousness is perhaps what I want to say.

As far as poetry that sketches collective consciousness – systems of oppression felt in the face of, e.g., colonial destruction, it may be seen as didactic, or perhaps it's just a different valence of private experience; one's private experience of the violence done to one's own people. Depending on the way the work is written it could be seen as didactic (teaching moment) but I do see that didacticism present in poetry that expresses private experience too – *here is my tragedy, I am alone with this, and there is no mentionable reason, but please empathize*; *here is my tow-headed child sitting in a patch of sunlight with our new kitten. I want to tell you how vulnerable they are.*

The private can be political, though?

Yes, in a way I have created a false dilemma. I have been reading Mahmoud Darwish's *Memory for Forgetfulness*. As Beirut is terrorized, as the bombs drop, we are invited into the poet's daily ritual of coffee preparation, for instance. The personal minutia here meets the larger canvas of terror, despair, imperialist assault.

There are lots of examples from Mahmoud Darwish of the private experience of living under occupation and settler-colonialism. In reader-response criticism, we may not wish to use those sociological/political terms and focus instead on the poet's craft, aspects of the way the personal is sketched. Another example of this kind of expression is found in the recently translated poems of Maya Abu al-Hayyat, *You Can Be the Last Leaf* (translated by Fady Joudah). In her review of that collection, Lena Khalaf Tuffaha writes,

Despite her belief in art 'as reparation for love and wisdom', Abu Al-Hayyat's poems remain firmly planted in the realities of a colonized homeland. In 'Massacres', the state of siege that marks all Palestinian life is laid bare:

Massacres teach me not to wait for
those who'll be pulled out of the rubble
and not to follow the stories of survivors.
I go on with my day without pausing for wonders.

How has this affected your own work and thinking?

On my quest to find an alternative to the Strong Voice of an Individual, ironically, I turned to the idea of identity. One's identity as a person with Indigenous roots opens a political or a justice consciousness, questions that perforce move us beyond individuation. There is a collective consciousness. That led me to an interest in the history of one side of my family, the Palestinian side. As soon as I started to learn more about the people in my family it was impossible to separate them from the wider history of the Palestinian people in the nineteenth and twentieth centuries. I couldn't write about my family members without realizing that the fragmented nature of their recollections, and the elliptical nature of what could be known about them – the knowledge of them that I could shore up – was inextricably bound to the wider history of colonial violence and anti-colonial resistance to European imperialist designs on the Levant region, the *bilad a-sham.*

It was startling, then, to read Edward Said's description of Palestinian literature: 'Our characteristic mode… is not a narrative in which scenes take place *seriatim*, but rather broken narratives, fragmentary compositions, and self-consciously staged testimonials in which the narrative voice keeps stumbling over itself, its obligations and its limitations (Said, *After the Last Sky*).

As I read books on the history of Al Quds (Jerusalem) and travelled in Palestine, I came across many mentions, people, places from the photos in those books, and from the stories my father told me. The street wall, in the photo of my father outside his home before the Nakba… was right there, miraculously, outside the window of my hotel when I visited for the first time in early 2020. The photo is dated 1945. How strange to see the bullet holes in the aluminium wall in front of a girls grammar school that my father mentioned, in real life, as I walked beside it in his former neighbourhood. How strange to discover an archive of unpublished *National Geographic* photos on Instagram and find many members of my own family in 1974, in the house not yet demolished in the Old City. Apparently, it stood alongside three other houses, as late as 1974, following Israel's ethnic cleansing and destruction of the rest of the neighbourhood – the twelfth-century Mughrabi (Moroccan) Quarter – in 1967.

Pieces of oneself, one's family, in history, in documentation, and in real life. This has affected my poetic consciousness, though it is surely not uniquely Palestinian. I don't know. Mostly it is this return to history – and literal return to the land in the case of Palestine – that directs my poems because this larger reality is impossible to ignore given the forced displacement of the Palestinian people. There is a throughline running from every Palestinian's life to the *Nakba* (catastrophe). The 'lost ground of our origins' is forever discoverable in writing and perceiving.

The phrase enables us to begin to scratch the surface of the potentialities of Indigenous poetries; writing from the condition of exile or the loss of ground – the land – where Indigenous people belong, recuperates the seeds of revolution that would up-end settler-colonial culture and the belief in the nobility and purity of the settler-colony state and the culture of those who came in the wake of those imperialist invasions. No wonder Canadian state media, the CBC, told my publisher that *Resisting Canada* 'is not for us', and would not give it any attention.

To be honest I am not sure to what extent I have at all been affected stylistically in my own work except to say that I prefer to write about this stuff through fiction and non-fiction rather than poetry. I am not sure why. Poetry of the kind I wrote in *Sumptuary Laws* is rooted in grandiloquence, lyricism, bombast, mannered poses, decorative excess, rhyme and alliteration, nursery rhymes and nonsense verse, and my imitative/parodic assay on high aesthetics and stylized writings. My inspirations were Wallace Stevens, Elizabeth Bishop and T.S. Eliot, for instance; Ashbery, Mlinko and others.

Whatever poetry I have so far written about Palestine has been rooted in my extensive reading of its history – particularly the last 150 years. This period of colonialism on Palestine is arguably the most brutal, according to the historian and researcher Salman Abu-Sitta. At this time, on social media and elsewhere on any given day, one witnesses video footage of Palestinians defending their land against settlers and the Israeli forces that work to protect illegal activity the settlers carry out as deputized agents of the state. The settler activity is no different than that of the settlers who were deputized to steal land from Indigenous Peoples in North America, Turtle Island. The *Nakba* begun against the Palestinian people in 1947–8 has not stopped.

I don't think I've found a way to express all this in poetry to my satisfaction, as if writing poetry for me, begun as something quite other, cannot now be transposed to 'history from below'. Of course, many poets have expressed dispossession quite beautifully. I'm thinking for instance of Lena Khalaf Tuffaha's 'Mountain, Stone' from her collection *Water & Salt*:

Do not name your daughters Shaymaa,
courage will march them
into the bullet path of dictators.

Do not name them Sundus,
the garden of paradise calls out to its marigolds,
gathers its green leaves up in its embrace.

Do not name your children Malak or Raneem,

angels want the companionship of others like them,
their silvery wings trailing the filth of jail cells,
the trill of their laughter a call to prayer.

Do not name your sons Hamza.
Do not taunt the torturer's whip
with promises of steadfastness.

Do not name your sons
Muhammad Ahed Zakaria Ismail,
they will become seashells, disappear in the sand.

Do not name your children. Let them live
nameless, seal their eyelids
and sell their voices to the nightingale.

Do not name your children
and if you must
call them by what withstands

this endless season of decay.
Name them mountains,
call them stone.

I'm also thinking of Mahmoud Darwish's *In the Presence of Absence* and *Mural*. The Gaza scholar and writer Haider Eid has described his own process in literature seminars as a mode of inquiry springing from the standpoint of the colonized and how it provides an alternative to the official, i.e. more dominant version of history of the colonizer. 'We then compare Palestinian and South African history and conclude that Apartheid and Zionism both created a dominant historical narrative that sought to eliminate all other narratives.' (Eid, *Mondoweiss*, 2022). In this way, poetry is also political consciousness, knowledge.

The definition of Said's that you began with is Eliotic – that's 'The Waste Land'. How might your own poem, 'On Palaces', fit into this discussion?

'On Palaces' was written in part about Orient House, located in East Jerusalem on Abu Obeida Street, a house that belongs to the Husaynis, a political class elite Jerusalem dynasty – perhaps to be considered Palestinian nobility. The Orient House served later as the headquarters of the Palestine Liberation Organization, until 2001, when it was seized by the Israelis and looted of historic documents. I read about it in a book on Jerusalem and came to see the site on my visit in 2020; in the same book, I found evidence of family members, for example a great-uncle who was for decades a football and athletic coach at the nearby St George's School and the Friends School in Ramallah. The whole family – the men, anyway – attended St George's. There are other landmarks in the area too, a couple of palaces bearing my great-grandmother's surname and presumably being owned by her family, and so on.

So, I think my stumbling, to borrow Said's idea, my fragmentary narrative, to think on Eliot, is larger history as a backdrop for the fragments I have shored against my, or my familial, ruins. I have picked up other fragments

reading other texts, as well, such as the role my elders played in the Battle of Sheikh Jarrah of 1948, an important site of resistance that could be considered the theatre of Palestinian victory against Zionist incursions on Al Quds. I know about these people because they are directly connected to relatives in Canada – this too is the fragment, embodied. The looting and other history recounted in 'On Palaces' traces the importance of materiality to the colonial condition – this history is directly connected to people, to papers, archives, stone and mortar. It's through a materialist historical framework that we can best understand the machinations of imperial violence and trace that violence on the land – including urban places – to the attempted erasure of a people. Many of the funeral processions of prominent Palestinians martyred in 1948 began at the Orient House. In 1949, it served as the headquarters the United Nations Relief and Works Agency (UNRWA), a United Nations office specifically created in the wake of the transformation of so many Palestinians living in their own homeland to 'Palestine refugees'. Again, this history cements the condition of being Palestinian in concrete ways.

What is the connection for you between poetry and history?

Knowing one's history lends authenticity to one's narratives – one's personal history but, equally importantly, the history of one's roots – how one's family arrived at the place they were at when one was a child, experiencing everything for the first time. If, as the American poet Louise Glück has written, 'we see the world once, in childhood' / the rest is memory', what lurks in that memory? The memory of my mother's high cheekbones and almond-shaped eyes, for instance, might draw me to the characteristic physiognomy of her people, in Central Asia, the mountains north of Kabul and the region of Bokhara. Under what colonial conditions do those people live, today? How has the present condition been established?

I do not mean to cancel the idea of a mannered, or stylish form of expression when I say we strive for authenticity; rather that there is a buttress, a scaffolding that history provides for the creative expression of poetry, narrative arts, and other types of language art. It is out of social conditions that art is produced, not really out of some disengaged and dematerialized encounter of a divine nature. The poet is not outside of the conditions of history. There are material conditions and cause and effect that may connect poetry with history. I say this in contradistinction to German Romanticism; not, perhaps, in opposition to Wordsworth.

Is understanding of history then a way to create a poem that doesn't sound touristic? 'On Palaces' certainly doesn't, yet it has that element to it.

Sometimes, as in the Palestinian case which is once again pertinent to your broader inquiry, one may witness what has happened *only* as a tourist, not only because one may not have access to normally accessible archival material (so much of Palestine's records were destroyed or remain confiscated), but because the trauma of the *Nakba* means that it can be very difficult to ask those who lived through it – now quite elderly – to produce an oral history. Luckily, the latter exists anyway, in recorded narratives. As far as I'm aware, these are mostly rendered in Arabic. Millions of Palestinians are not permitted to enter Palestine at all, so they can't even go to their ancestral homeland as tourists. Many in Gaza and Lebanon camps live in walking distance or a short drive from the homes they were forced to flee. They are barred and remain in those camps waiting for their inalienable right of return to be granted. Return, *'al-awda'*, is the heart of the Palestine matter.

The aspiration of being a returnee surpasses 'witness' and 'tourist'. I think one can sound like a tourist – enter the territory as a tourist – and still have an understanding of history, still become a witness. Being a tourist may sound less authentic, but if you are a tourist with blood ties and historic belonging, then it may be that one's tourism feels like something more profound, i.e., being a witness. My own experience of being in Sheikh Jarrah, reading about my relatives' roles in the Battle of Sheikh Jarrah in 1948, and two years after my visit, watching video on Twitter of the same battle continuing, added another dimension to the act of being a witness. The personal is political.

You mentioned above that you prefer fiction and non-fiction for your writings on Palestine, yet '1948', a newer poem, has its declarations and intentions, 'Who spoke before the planners of towers, private agencies? / Before mandate, civilizing committee, Declaration, / billionaire American, capital, and colony hotel? / All the implementations that do not suffer metaphor.' And its own music and mannerisms, especially around polysyllabic language.
Your work suggests the two things can mix in poetry.

I find it difficult to write about serious subjects using the conventions of English poetry – rhyming couplets, for instance. This is not to say that some formal devices might not work very well in formal register – the villanelle, for instance, even the pantoum. When I think of the sound making the sense, I think of wonder about, e.g., a seashell, the sunlight striking the underside of clouds, the sound of waves, a spring morning of damp grass and robins. Maybe I have chosen trite examples; but I place wonder into a separate category from rumination. Awe or even Wordsworth's emotion recollected

in tranquility, is not the same as rumination, anger, resistance against the nexus of imperial power trying to destroy you or steal your home. And so I arrived at the idea that I prefer fiction or non-fiction prose for such expression. But clearly many poets excel with this, so it's really a reflection on my limits! Matthew Arnold would disagree.

Are there limits to what a poem can do, you think?

One can use language in thousands of ways – perhaps this is limitless. But language is 'always already', it is always removed from the immediacy of a happening. It can record, it records after the fact. To inhabit it is to admit to a deadened condition. It's dead, there on the page recounting what happened off the page. For these reasons it's a powerful or maybe I could say homeopathic conduit for expressing trauma, which we might twin with shame – always hidden and removed from view and from the present. I am thinking of the long poem in D.M. Thomas's *The White Hotel*, where history, both personal and shared, is a major element.

In an essay he based on the introduction to his translation of Jan Zábrana's *The Lesser Histories*, Justin Quinn wrote:

W.B. Yeats was surely wrong when he wrote that '[w]e make out of the quarrel with others, rhetoric, but of the quarrel with ourselves, poetry.' This suggests that poetry, in its essence, has no public dimension, that the realms of politics, of community, of shared experiences more generally, don't belong in the genre, which is better suited to expressions of the inner spirit. Of course, the first place to look for evidence that Yeats was wrong is in his own poetry. Many of his poems resonated, and still resonate, in public forums, while others that talk of love and of spirit make some fine rhetorical moves. Still, the dictum can't quite be discounted, as it suggests that poetry can somehow reach deeper into the spirit than any other literary genre.

I don't buy that dictum because I've read countless beautiful sentences, and their beauty moved me as much as lineated cadence. They were in fiction, in criticism, in essays... probably even newspaper articles.

The Wood of the Suicides

GARETH PRIOR

I'd found myself in a forest, trackless, lit
by shadows. Flashback: tumbling into sleep,
slumped on a book where *Nessus hadn't yet*

returned to the other side I woke to trip
headlong through *thorns* and *dark leaves* in some savage
thicket of multiplying authorship –

and just as a dream's blurred overlay can merge
disparate loves: translations, parallel text,
commentary, imitations all converge

on the place I wandered, terrified, perplexed
where *harpies...make lament on the strange trees*
and pain severed in one life grafts the next.

Barely a few steps on, the gloom was worse –
everywhere wailing, indistinct as air
until a voice broke off: 'I'd recognise

that slouching *faux*-detachment anywhere.
I knew you as a serious boy when sandstone
glowed like false memory summer-long, the spire

conjuring mist and bell-notes: we were children
playing at everything, lost, in love with words –
thinking the world was ours and ours alone

and puffed-up with others' crap like "trod the boards",
"*amor* reflected", "myth", "semantic field".
But that was another century, and besides

I'm dead. Tell me what's happening with the wild
carnival I once knew – and why you've strayed
before your time into the unlit world.'

She wasn't there: *the way unseasoned firewood
spits from one end* and hisses through the grate,
that's how the tree had spoken, but I answered:

'When we saw *Tristan*, 1998
you told me over drinks you'd only cried
because the last act made *being* seem too great

a burden for one person (though denied
as quickly as you'd said it). Things moved on.
Those we both love recounted how you died.'

She sighed: 'How can you even parse the pain
of that decision? Compassion mixed with blame:
your choice is easy – fail or fail again,

renounce your magic, write – it's not the same
as *be* or *not,* fleeing the mind's own rough
music. Self can be slipped off like a name,

the urge remains – chasing success through life
white-hot with need you'd never understand.
Nothing (and now not even that) was enough.

You know the rest: I left the world behind,
cleared every choice but one and leapt to meet
the train that was always hurtling to that end.

A life sentence commuted to nothing.' Light
as loss, the day beckoned me on: no trace
of my friend's voice remained. Unbroken night

held that *dark wood* untouched by *sun* or *stars.*

Reviews

Blaise Cendrars

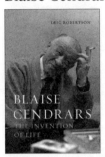

Eric Robertson, *Blaise Cendrars: The Invention of Life*
(Reaktion Books) £25
Reviewed by Roger Little

Anyone interested in the numerous French literary and artistic movements of the earlier part of the twentieth century will have appreciated Eric Robertson's penetrating earlier contributions to a deeper critical understanding of the many '-isms' of the period and some of their outstanding practitioners. The interaction of the verbal and the visual lies at the heart of his interests, expressed in studies of Cubism, Dada, Futurism, Surrealism, Situationism and major works on Arp and Miró. Blaise Cendrars (1887–1961), who constantly reinvented himself through his writings, from the early poetry to the late autobiographical novels, is the subject of this admirably researched and engaging study.

Some of the terms used in my opening paragraph require qualification, mostly because they are too limiting: 'French' extends beyond France, in this case to Switzerland, where 'Blaise Cendrars', originally Frédéric Louis Sauser, was born; 'novels' is a problematic label for the narrative tetralogy he wrote in the 1940s. 'Boundaries mean nothing to me' might hark back to Aristophanes' *The Birds* but remains entirely relevant to Cendrars. Generic boundaries, but also geographical ones. By the age of seventeen he was in Russia, by twenty-four in the United States, by thirty-seven in Brazil, each time for lengthy stays. That wonderful word 'bourlinguer', which I first learned from Cendrars more years ago than I care to remember, showed him already on a roll. This is indeed 'experience as flux'.

Robertson lays out his ambition clearly:

Across its very considerable breadth, Cendrars's literary œuvre is surprisingly homogeneous; it has myriad facets and employs many different literary modes, but it does so with a single, unmistakeable voice. [...] The book asks to what extent it is possible to consider Cendrars's extensive literary output as a continuous whole.

He builds on the essential groundwork done by Claude Leroy and his team, responsible first for the fifteen-volume *Œuvres complètes* (2000–6) and then for the magisterial four-volume Pléiade edition of the *Œuvres autobiographiques complètes* (2013) and the *Œuvres romanesques* (2017).

The early poetry (1912–13) was both stunningly modern and immensely influential: *Pâques à New York* and *La Prose du Transsibérien et de la Petite Jehanne de France*, the latter here being reproduced in colour to make available, in miniature, the text enhanced by Sonia Delaunay's swirls of colour. With typical enthusiasm, Robertson deems it to be 'a staggeringly audacious, radically experimental and ravishingly beautiful work of art'. Cendrars's collaboration with artists was to continue, notably with Fernand Léger, but it extended further when he became involved with film-making (Abel Gance) and photography (Robert Doisneau), such popular arts confirming his anti-elitist stance as part of his 'hybrid aesthetic'. Maps are a significant feature, incorporated for instance in *Le Panama*, covering the expanses of America; Robertson seems surprised when Paris is mentioned in that poem, but Paris was familiarly known as 'Paname' at the time and Cendrars, whose base it was from 1912, would have been sensitive to the echo.

In September 1915, a year into the First World War, Cendrars's right arm was shot to pieces. It was a defining moment in his life and work as was that war in world history, though the event is scarcely mentioned in his writings, even in *La Main coupée*. But where would his writing have gone after *Dix-neuf poèmes élastiques*, composed before the war but published after it? What are here presented as 'strings of disparate images devoid of connecting phrases or any obvious unifying semantic field' look forward, I think, to late Beckett, as in *Not I*, at the limits of communication and yet powerful in their intensity. Returning to Paris in 1917 after a period of convalescence, he made significant friends while remaining 'very firmly an individualist': Apollinaire, Cocteau, Satie, Stravinsky and others, sparking off a major new phase of creativity. It involves 'bricolage, collage, montage, citations and even plagiarism' and a modernist 'aesthetics of accumulation' in its refusal to produce 'high literature'.

In 1925, with his first novel, Cendrars struck gold: *L'Or*, 'an exhilarating and compelling read', was his greatest commercial success. The sprawling 'multilayered textual artefact' of *Moravagine*, 'an act of literary bravura' 'baroque in its excess', followed in 1926:

> In turns gently poetic and uncompromisingly experimental, violent and violently funny, action-packed and quietly contemplative, this novel is infuriating, perplexing, yet still breathtakingly original. It conveys an unremittingly bleak vision of humanity through the protagonists' journey of violent and relentless destruction; yet it does so through the author's orchestration of an extraordinary patchwork of textual matter.

I cite this passage partly as an example of the author's infectious enthusiasm for his subject. But the etymology of 'enthusiasm' carries a health warning. I am minded of W.S. Gilbert's line in *The Gondoliers* that 'when everyone is somebody, then no one's anybody'. Cendrars's varied and variable work is somewhat flattened out in this book, as if Robertson shied away from being judgemental. It is the one reservation that I have about this excellent and hugely informative study. Could it, as so often happens, have been influenced by its subject? Cendrars made 'no qualitative distinction between fifteenth-century poetry, ancient religious writings and popular serial novels'. I recognise, however, that it is a cordial invitation to explore Cendrars's writings and to come to one's own decisions about its polyphonic reinventions, its willing, sometimes wilful confusion of fact and fiction.

The autofictional tetralogy published in the 1940s – *L'Homme foudroyé*, *La Main coupée*, *Bourlinguer* and *Le Lotissement du ciel* (not *The Allotment of the Sky* as translated here but rather *The Estate in the Sky* in the sense of a housing estate – is Cendrars's last major literary undertaking. Among the 'expansive digressions, philosophical passages, entertaining anecdotes, asides to the reader and scholarly notes' are numerous pointers to the writer's life, their credibility questioned by their context: 'we are left with the impression that the writing self has been reduced to a camera of sorts, registering scenes mechanically but unable to process them'. Robertson, far from being disconcerted, sees virtues in such quasi-cinematographic writing. His conclusion stresses the diversity of Cendrars's output but sees it 'united by a spirit of innovation and an irrepressible energy'. '[F]or him, the act of writing should be unfettered and should not pin its colours to any rigid political, literary, aesthetic or ideological mast'. His particular form of modernity 'stems from the belief that living is as important as writing and much more valuable than theorizing'.

I have no quarrel with that and spare you the occasional quibble over points of translation and the like. Such details are of little consequence in this welcome presentation of a major, if complex and enigmatic figure in modernist literature, brought from the margins to centre-stage in this well-produced and important study rounded off by a substantial bibliography and a good index.

Spiritual Verse

The Penguin Book of Spiritual Verse: 110 Poets on the Divine, Kaveh Akbar, editor (Penguin Classics) £20
Reviewed by Rachel Mann

I am unsure if a poetry editor is a kind of god, but in order to do their job well they must deliver judgment on the living and, when curating an anthology of this sort, on the dead too. As Kaveh Akbar notes in his introduction to this rich and varied volume, the earliest attributable author in all of human literature is an ancient Sumerian priestess named Enheduanna. Across four and a half thousand years, she speaks of awe and ecstasy, of body and the Divine, and concludes, 'Even my sex is dust'. The ancient dead know things and deliver their judgment on those, like me, who inspect their words in search of good news.

I am struck by Akbar's decision to call this a book of 'spiritual verse' rather than 'religious poetry'. Does it matter? Probably not. Indeed, the decision displays practical wisdom. In such times as these, when – even for religious people like me – the word 'religious' has acquired connotations of overweening piety, 'spiritual' is a sufficiently expansive term to ensure this book has greater reach and, in turn, saleability. More seriously, as David Jones noted, 'religious' implies a commitment and connection to something definite in a way that 'spiritual' does not: ligament and religion, Jones noted, arise from the same Latin root, 'religio'. That which is religious, then, provides connective tissue between word, practice, and a usually unseen Divine.

I commend Akbar's decision-making regarding which poets to include and exclude. It is exquisite and reflects the richness of world literature; Akbar is catholic in his selection and he resists Eurocentric notions of value. He reveals, if a reader did not already know, that where there has been human society there have been poets prepared to speak into what Lucille Clifton called 'the lip of our understanding'. I know that in Akbar's place I should have been paralysed by the sheer breadth of choice. Nonetheless, I was sad to see that neither Christina Rossetti nor Jones himself made the cut. Perhaps their poems, especially Rossetti's later work and Jones' *Anathemata*, speak too much of the religious and insufficiently of the spiritual. Their writing resists the (post-) modern, liberal person's longing to appropriate a text to their own spiritual ends.

Gilles Deleuze, after Spinoza, said, 'we do not know what the body can do'. Many of the poems included in this anthology test the limits of what may be said or known of bodies. That should not be surprising. If the word 'spiritual' has been degraded by overuse (you know something is up when TV ads sell us things like yoghurt on the basis of vague spiritual aspirations), it is most properly located in the dynamics of a body as it seeks to make sense of its longings, its bewilderment, or its hope. The writer of the Song of Songs says, 'A bundle of myrrh is my wellbeloved unto me; he shall lie all night betwixt my breasts'. Myrrh, that symbol of death, becomes in addition a symbol of a beloved body brought alive in the realm of sex. In 'Homage to Claudius Ptolemy', Octavio Paz writes, 'I'm man: I exist briefly / and the night is enormous. / But I look up: / the stars write. / Without understanding I get it: / I'm writing too / and in this very instant / someone is spelling me out.' Akbar says this of that one line, 'Without understanding I get it': it is a 'distillation of all the poets in this volume'. A poet or a priestess or a supplicant writes, and words shade in one direction or another. In one direction they shade towards poetry and in another towards liturgy; sometimes one cannot distinguish between them and, I guess, when that happens a religion may be born.

Does spiritual verse necessarily take us away from the demotic? One might say, what else is its purpose if not to resist and reformulate the commonplace? The Iraqi poet Nazik Al-Malaika writes, 'Our life we have dedicated as a prayer / To whom will we pray... but to words?' Akbar's selection of poems reminds me repeatedly that if poets wrestle with the improbability that there are any words at all rather than nothing, spiritual verse finds – to use that phrase of Herbert's – 'heaven in ordinary'. If this sounds like a kind of pietism, such writing need not become such. This anthology includes the most remarkable selection of poets who, in the midst of persecution or torment, find words which reformulate the language of political commitment. Akbar includes the Jewish mystical poet Edmond Jabès's interrogative poem, 'At the Threshold of the Book'. Jabès asks, '"What is the story of the book?" / "Becoming aware of a scream."' He reframes the violence of centuries in two lines. Anna Akhmatova's *Requiem* speaks of state violence through the line of Christ's crucifixion and draws a bleak conclusion: 'I'd like to name them all by name, / But the list has been confiscated and is nowhere to be found.'

The above should not make a reader think the anthology settles for a minor key. If, as a theologian once claimed, 'God is in the facts', Akbar's selection ultimately reminds me that spiritual verse dares to take the risk of mockery, not least because its defining mode is praise. Inrasara, the contemporary Vietnamese poet, encourages writers to waste time. Speaking of his abiding passion, Cham poetry, he says: 'I want to squander my entire life on it... though there may only be one person / or even if there's not a single soul.'

The word 'verse', of course, finds its origins in the notion of a line; it has implications of turning or plough-

ing a field as well as of writing poetry. I think there is dignity in committing to the practice of spiritual verse: it invites us to see such writing as a ploughing up of the field of the Divine. Only then might a poet who wishes to treat with God be ready to attempt something greater. As Al-Malaika says: 'Tomorrow we will build ourselves a dream-nest of words.'

David Wevill

David Wevill, *Collected Earlier Poems* and *Collected Later Poems* (Shearsman) both £17.95
Reviewed by Ian Pople

While it is inevitable to invoke Ted Hughes when considering the poetry of David Wevill – and not only because of Hughes's ill-fated relationship with Wevill's wife, Assia – it is also a lazy comparison. Wevill has, after all, had a career in poetry which is both prolific in its own way and has been, in terms of chronology, longer lasting. The problem is that Wevill, although born in Canada and long domiciled in Texas, started that career in the UK. As the publishers, Shearsman themselves, note, 'While resident in England in the 1950s and '60s, [Wevill] established a substantial reputation as a poet, publishing four volumes between 1964 and 1973. He won prizes, was represented in major anthologies such as *The New Poetry* and *A Group Anthology,* and was included in the renowned *Penguin Modern Poets* series before his first full collection appeared.' None of which, of course, aligns Wevill with Hughes per se. But open almost any page of the first two books collected in the *Collected Earlier Poems* and it feels almost impossible not to view them through the perspective of our received notion of what Hughes was doing.

I wonder how possible it will be to read Wevill's 'Black Pantheress' without Hughes' Jaguar pacing up and down its cage and staring back at you. And yet, and yet... Wevill initially places the live pantheress in the landscape among the jungle, the monsoon, 'under the loud stars at night, or by / thick cordwood heaped for winter in the hills / where ice struck.' But, as we learn at the end of the first part of the poem, the panther's desire for peace, with which the poem begins, ends with 'A home-made village gun, / her stretcher a long pole'. And the dreams of peace have Wevill's 'neighbour' the pantheress a 'coffin'. Wevill then turns the poem, 'She is the eye's / black pupil; and the still / blind spot in a man's eye gazing / directly at God, seeing nothing.' 'Black Pantheress' is from Wevill's 1966 volume, *A Christ of the Ice-Floes*. And we might think that such writing has been heavily drenched in Hughes. But this book predates *Crow* by three years. If Wevill has imbibed Hughes, and in particular the poems that Hughes would put in 1967's *Wodwo,* perhaps, it is actually possible to drive the influence of those poems further.

The *Collected Earlier Poems* ends with the poem and prose sequence 'Where the Arrow Falls'. These poems, too, reach for the mythic. They use, the blurb tells us, elements of a Hopi creation story, and the poems themselves explore with real eloquence what it means to be both a parent and a child. Towards the end of the sequence, Wevill writes, 'World was whatever he could get his hands on that was not him, but that could become him if he exerted all his energy and bore down on it.' This sense of sheer greed for the world is something that runs through Wevill's writing from the start to the end of these two volumes.

Wevill's *Collected Later Poems* is no less extensive than the first volume, although the voice becomes sparer, slightly thinner. If the investment in the world is just as great, it is an investment in a somewhat more personal world. In the later poems, the I is more prominent. The I is the authorising consciousness of the poems with the emphasis rather more on the 'authorising.' This makes the poems no less plangent, but occasionally the reader might feel that the poems are more 'political' with a small 'p'. That greed for the world is just as urgent if a little more focused on the self in the world.

In the brief sequence of three, unrhymed fourteen-liners for 'Jeanne D'Arc', from Wevill's 1994 collection *Child Eating Snow,* these elements are finely balanced into a beautiful and imaginative engagement with the French saint; 'I see her wandering among the trees, a / paradox of incommutable light / in the forest about the house. Her fingers trail the wind / through spider hangings where little leaves get caught.' And Wevill finishes the sequence with the lines, 'There will come a morning when everything seems clear / I imagine: when the clenched hand of fire opens / and releases you. And we can breathe again.' The inclusion of that 'I imagine' seems finely judged. It halts the progress of the syntax for a moment and both acknowledges the potential artifice of the making but also the human engagement thus making the saint more human, too.

The final sequence of *Collected Later Poems* is called 'Asterisks'. This is a group of forty-nine short-lined and short poems written in a bitten, almost wheezing style. There is a tanka-like directness to both the imagery and the energy of the poems. This is number thirty-five: 'When a poem goes for a walk / it whistles up the neighbour's dog, / it breathes a thousand smells. // Tree, who are you / to tell me I'm not one. // Smoke over the river // Sun gone down.' These two *Collected*s gather up a considerable and compelling achievement.

Huge Dolls Get Mandolined

Poppy, Joseph Minden (Carcanet) £11.99
Reviewed by Horatio Morpurgo

The paintings in Anselm Kiefer's recent retrospective, 'Pour Paul Celan', centred around the large lead sculpture of a 1940s aircraft. Its wings were loaded with lead books, their pages marked with poppy heads on long stems, of the same metal. These unlikely book-marks were not a reference to poppies as the British might think of them in connection with war. They were a quotation from 'Mohn und Gedächtnis' / 'Poppy and Memory', an early poem of Celan's in which this pair figure as inseparable antagonists rather than synonyms.

Joseph Minden's collection goes potholing deep below the familiar surface of such imagery. 'In 1960 / the Imperial War Graves Commission / changed its name', as he baldly puts it, prefacing a story. In November 2010 a British delegation to China, led by Prime Minister David Cameron, was asked to remove the poppies they were wearing, as to their hosts these were 'reminders of the Opium War'. The poppies were not removed.

What exactly do we remember through poppies and who is this 'we'? Minden's 'Edwardian headwound... re-opens as a memorial in 1920' to be used as a 'hospital serving poppies... in the form of strong, forgetful tea'. Or again, remembrance is an 'anaesthetic haze / spreading like spilt tea across the map of the world'.

Poppies have another British history. They supplied a 'soft somniferum' that Celan would have recognised – for De Quincey as for Sara Coleridge and her 'nullifying cup / that terminates concern'. 'There are no headstones for what is under the name', Minden writes, lowering himself into the gulf fixed between what happened and what we commemorate.

A cheerful letter home is written in Penang by a sailor aboard the *Nemesis*, a heavily armed ship belonging to the East India Company. Bound for China in 1840, its weaponry and shallow draft will give it advantages of which it will make full use. The figure of 'Mina' recurs throughout the collection, the object of an enduring affection and the other half of an unresolved affair that mainly happened in Penang.

The 'anaesthetic haze' needs dispelling closer to home, too. 'The truth is not a headstone but a pit': in a war cemetery the poet imagines 'hundreds of white teeth turning in the eye of a red flower, whiteness misting to an uncountable array of red flowers'. There is no formula for redemption from history here, in private life or public.

'Re-enactment' is a fine sequence, each poem beginning with 'As I remember' and setting up a new 'you' and 'I' to go tumbling together a little further on through time and space, as well as back and forth across gender boundaries. King Arthur encounters evening traffic in Penang. Boudica meets a mug of cold tea. Prince Hal stops somewhere to eat with King Henry. 'I was hungry' he reflects, 'You were full. We stared past each other / the empty space between us like a mirror / or a time machine. You knew me / not.'

'Historical politics' is the university term for this and teams of graduate students are about it from Galway to Kharkhiv and beyond. As well they might be: our present and future are being determined by it to an alarming degree. When Minden sees populations 'transfixed before the clock face', he does more than any thesis can. With his Picardy 'where every Tory flashback starts' and his drunken British tourists staggering round small-town Belgium, he creates a memorable imagery for how the past is turned to corroborative nonsense. When he sees the 'growing mouth' or hears the 'building scream' beneath our feet he is warning, as poets are meant to.

Keats and Shelley

Kelvin Everest, *Keats and Shelley: Winds of Light* (OUP)
Reviewed by Judith Chernaik

A distinguished writer on all aspects of Romanticism, Kelvin Everest, chief editor of Longman's multi-volume edition of Shelley's poem, has been living closely with Shelley's manuscript drafts, fragments and completed texts since the 1980s. His unrivalled knowledge of these manuscripts gives special interest to the essays collected here, five on Keats, six on Shelley, with a close reading of *Adonais* linking the two halves of the collection.

Adonais beautifully illustrates the literary relations of the two poets. Keats's own poems are closely incorporated into Shelley's elegy: 'He is made one with Nature: there is heard / His voice in all her music, from the moan / Of thunder, to the song of night's sweet bird...' The final stanzas move from Keats to Shelley himself, elegist, mourner and fellow poet. The lines seem to prophecy Shelley's death by drowning when his sailboat capsized in the Gulf of Spezia: 'The breath whose might I have invoked in song / Descends on me; my spirit's bark is driven, / Far from

the shore, far from the trembling throng / Whose sails were never to the tempest given...'. Stanza xliv provides the dedication and subtitle of Everest's essays:

> ...When lofty thought
> Lifts a young heart above its mortal lair,
> And love and life contend in it, for what
> Shall be its earthly doom, the dead live there
> And move like winds of light on dark and stormy air.

Shelley argues here that art – poetry, lofty thought – survives its maker as 'winds of light' – inspiration and illumination. We can only agree, especially in our own 'dark and stormy' times. Keats believed that poetry offered a 'balm and comfort' to suffering humanity. Shelley was convinced that the 'electric fire' burning in the poetry of his own times predicted a vast change in society, approaching his own vision of a world 'Equal, unclassed, tribeless and nationless'. We still cherish the inspirational works of these young poets, the sonnets and odes so often anthologised, Keats's erotic romances, Shelley's political fables and pamphlets, his 'Defence of Poetry'. To our permanent loss, the ambitious works which might have defined their vision of art and life were left unfinished (Keats's *Fall of Hyperion,* Shelley's *Triumph of Life*). Keats died at twenty-five, Shelley just short of his thirtieth birthday.

Each of Everest's essays repays reading. In a move away from New Critical close reading of poetic texts, Everest discusses both poets in the context of their times – 'the literary, cultural, political and social currents of their age'. This approach serves Shelley well. The political views of a poet driven by his 'passion for reforming the world' have probably spoken more clearly to readers than anything else in his works. Keats is very different. He could be arguing against Shelley in the moral he attaches to the Grecian Urn: 'Beauty is truth, truth beauty – that is all / Ye know on earth, and all ye need to know.'

Yet as Everest argues, Keats too is a poet of his times. His poetic inspirations included not only Chapman's Homer, Shakespeare and Milton, but Wordsworth, whose 'Excursion' he considered one of the three things 'to rejoice at in this age'. He conceived at one point of becoming a political journalist, 'on the liberal side'. As a medical student at Guy's Hospital, he had more direct experience of the misery of his age – 'The weariness, the fever, and the fret / Here, where men sit and hear each other groan' – than Shelley, who was protected by a privileged education and an assured income.

In addition to Everest's expertise as editor, his close readings of individual poems are suggestive. He must have inspired generations of students with his own love of literature – a special gift, which underpins his scholarship. It's a pleasure to share this generous selection of his work.

Oems

oems, Matthew Tomkinson (Guernica Editions) $20 CAD
Reviewed by Greg Thomas

Matthew Tomkinson's *oems* is a sequence of thirty-six lipogrammatic poems that omit all 'ascending or descending elements' (hence its title, excluding the downward-thrusting *p*). In the post-free-verse universe there perhaps remains a kneejerk assumption that any such exercise must be a matter of righteous self-efface-ment, of abdicating authorship to algorithm, purging the written page of the interpolated and debased lyric 'I'. But Tomkinson's compositional method actually springs directly from the hinterland of that 'I,' docu-menting and exorcising his experiences of OCD (a more ravaging condition than the flippant social-media use of the term would imply).

As such, *oems* can be read both as a series of playful, mind-flexing exercises in constrained composition and as the displaced expression of something deeper, more emotionally compelling, and more human. Before expanding on that point, however, lets explore the ter-rain of Tomkinson's flatlands. Thematically speaking, his poems run a surprising gamut: there are, perhaps predictably, self-reflexive ruminations on the method ('an excisor – a remover / a voracious eraser / a manicure – a circumcision'). But there are also neat little language games touching on the psychology of art and film ('cin-ema / zeroes in on / essences // essences / are / recursive // recursive / means / cocoa in a mirror // a mirror / is a canvas / as seen in meninas'). There are impossibly squeezed-out narrative and polemic sequences – 'mini-mise avariceness / rove oversize casinos / commence inversion' – and little anti-imperialist graffitos: 'erasure / is a / war crime // evenness / means / massacres // u.s.a vows / concussive rain / summons zeus'. Each poem, in other words, is bounded by subject matter as well as by the parameters of a particular sorting method. At times, we're treated to some homophonic feints that ask us to think using our mind's ear as well as its eye ('resume – résumé / sewers – sewers / sow – sow').

Broadly speaking, in a world where advertising and even political discourse is governed by the insights of covert data mining on a grand scale, there's something resonant about a poetics that places the obsessive tram-melling and scouring of information front and centre. Tomkinson leans into the association with his twen-ty-seventh poem, a list of website names: 'amazon.com / news.com / xxx.com'. Then again, this is mining as per-formed by a single human mind, and it's really as a

covert expression of selfhood that *oems* appeals. The tortuous, rule-based prose that it sometimes put me in mind of – Perec's *La Disparition*, Beckett's *Watt* – docu-mented the traumas and deprivations of World War Two. The terms here aren't comparable, of course, but there's something of the same maddening, exhilarating, cathar-tic energy to Tomkinson's collection. It's something dif-ferent, and something worthwhile.

Artist and Poet

Lucy Rose Cunningham *Interval: House, Lover, Slippages* (Broken Sleep Books) £8.50
Reviewed by Anthony Barnett

Lucy Rose Cunningham is an artist and a poet. Her stud-ies and her degree are in art but I believe she sees herself as a poet first. *Interval* is posited as her first book, fol-lowing a chapbook, *Mary, Marie, Maria: after the nectar, pyre and linden tree*, from the same publisher. As her titles might suggest, Cunningham often writes in what I like to call wide expanses. That was also evident in her uncollected debut work in *Snow lit rev*, although *Interval* is composed of semi-discrete shorter lyrics.

It is no surprise that lockdown has generated a great many poems (to say nothing of illnesses, and other writ-ing and the arts). Lockdown, from 2020, followed by *Days are opening up*, are the occasions for *Interval* but not the be-all, and that is refreshing. There are humorous asides: 'I want to hold you / but the line's busy.' Or *En route to Morrison's*, though, knowing the author, not for the lambs' chops: 'Red Sky at night. Shoppers' delight.' But in *Memories have such delicate membranes* serious-ness steps in, as it does most everywhere: 'She added them to her shelf, / precariously handling preciousness.'

There is a sort of giveaway: 'When I search for words to *protect*, / our thesaurus reads *inoculate*.' Is there a rhyme there? It feels as if there is. A delicate balance. Nowhere is there any sense other than that a true word has been found, if it has not already come to mind. Art is in the weather: *Today is a Rothko painting.* In a prose passage *Lead tin yellow.* 'they paint in. In cloth, light parts of the sky, and foliage. Vermeer saw A Lady Writing and sculpted her yellow drapery in such a pastel, imbu-ing cool blues with warm accents. Disarming yellow. Soft subtle poison. Lead tin yellow, like truth – visible, hard to swallow.'

It is not always clear whether an italic first line is truly a poem's title or simply a first line: some are followed by a line space, others are not. And their punctuation varies: a period, a comma, or nothing. I think it may be part of an orchestration. Disconcerting are a few section pages, and occasional strophes, in faint grey type. The greying is deliberate but so faint as to be nigh-on invisible. I wonder if the POD printing, which otherwise is good, is to blame.

None of that detracts from what is a delightful, clear-headed gathering of poems, almost innovative in the way Cunningham opens into her wide expanses (not easily reproducible partly because of some right margin alignment), in which the domestic, in the house and outside it, and the loving, are to the fore.

> *Thinking about break-ups in Folkestone,*
> *line after line of sundered conversation.*
>
> It's (too) late now, the tide floods in
> up deep gullies, muddy channels fill and the boats float off.
> White-caps break on the stone and not much else stirs.
>
> Idle, slow – the sea, its salt ancestral breathing
> murmuring back memories of life before.
> Great blue tutelar wrapping, embracing, relinquishing.
> Distance, we reach.

Prynne and Oliver

The Letters of Douglas Oliver and J.H. Prynne, 1967–2000, edited by Joe Luna (Amsterdam and Sofia: The Last Books) €25
Reviewed by Alex Latter

The correspondence collected together in this volume represents almost all of the letters exchanged between Douglas Oliver and J.H. Prynne. Oliver first made contact with Prynne in 1967, when he was working as a journalist at a local newspaper, asking to discuss some poems that he had recently written; the final letter here, from Prynne to Oliver, was sent a month before Oliver's death in April 2000, at the age of sixty-two.

It was not a steady correspondence. Bursts of exchange were often followed by months or years of near-silence. At its heart is a principled disagreement about the relationship between ethics, knowledge and poetic voice. As the correspondence continues, these issues come more clearly into focus. Some of the material, particularly early on, is pretty recondite. Scholarly references abound; the letters are thick with advanced mathemat-

ical and scientific lexicons, *pace* Prynne's description of Oliver's *The Harmless Building* as 'a three-dimensional endocrine hypersurface forming the world tube of the "novel"'.

Luna's glosses on the scholarly material – presented as marginal annotations rather than footnotes, and supported by a thorough introduction and well-chosen appendices – are assiduous, consistently enlightening and deployed with a lightness of touch that prevents them overwhelming the text. The difficult style is allowed to speak for itself. His introduction also acknowledges the additional difficulty presented by the 'capacity for unreflective, or indeed reflective, offensiveness' that is present in the 'scornful asides [and] casual stereotyping' found in both men's letters.

There is a lot here to be enjoyed though. All letters afford us glimpses of the lives being lived alongside the work being written; here, we see the itinerant Oliver shifting address – New York, Paris, Brightlingsea – and requesting references for jobs and funding applications while Prynne, ensconced at Gonville and Caius College, Cambridge, complains about marking. There are some very acute critical observations too. Oliver's account of Prynne's 'No Song No Supper' succinctly captures the power of Prynne's best poetry and the effect of 'its constant unexpectedness and juxtaposition of oddly comparable images creating a mysterious unity of field'. There is also humour, as in Prynne's self-deprecating take on *Bands Around the Throat* as 'a Reader's Digest version of the *Decline and Fall* on a handful of postcards'.

The correspondence is at its most memorable when Oliver and Prynne's disagreements are brought into sharpest relief. In an early letter, Prynne discerns an 'ethic vector' in Oliver's writing: the direction and magnitude of that vector is disputed, though, and the bulk of the correspondence here can be read as an attempt to work out the consequences of that dispute, both within their own writing and in the relationship between poetry and politics in its broadest sense.

If, as both men agree, 'speaking one's mind is a kind of delusion', what form of socially-oriented poetic utterance is possible? Following the election of the third Thatcher government in 1987, Prynne writes that 'the dream of ethical purpose answered formally is a fading relic' since it requires 'that we live in a stable order of decent, generous personal interconnection' whose terms are, he contends, in fact being 'reset, piece by piece'. For Oliver, though, in such a moment of apparent political hopelessness, 'the finest thing is to let literature live in hopeful purposes [...] because otherwise we deny everything life has always depended upon and we betray our fellow citizens'. Whereas Oliver contends that 'the enlarging of the I is better than its total abandonment', for Prynne, the ethic vector moves instead towards the diffraction of that self into often discontinuous discourses.

These letters set out the terms of this discussion very fully; their publication will enrich the appreciation and understanding of both Oliver and Prynne's work, and the contexts in which that work was written.

Roy Fisher

The Citizen and the Making of City, Roy Fisher, edited by Peter Robinson
(Bloodaxe) £14.99
Reviewed by Kyle Lovell

If you were to take the 907 bus from Sutton Coldfield into Birmingham city centre in the first few months of 2022, you would have found the journey fundamentally changing from week to week. It was on these bus rides, through the constant flux of a self-reconstructing city preparing for the Commonwealth Games, that I read Roy Fisher's *The Citizen and the Making of City*. Edited by Peter Robinson, the edition opens with the original manuscript of 'The Citizen' and gathers various versions of *City* together with Fisher's own commentary and other poems left in his estate.

Reproduced roughly sixty years after he 'finished' the unpublished manuscript that is the focal point of this publication, Fisher had earlier described 'The Citizen' in a letter to Gael Turnbull as a 'sententious prose book'. For me, it is a vividly incomplete collage of documentary and fictionalised encounters with(in) the city of Birmingham. Conversational, fragmented, anxious, voyeuristic, detached yet consistently attentive, this strange manuscript would be foundational to Fisher's poetics for years to come. Robinson outlines how 'The Citizen' influenced Fisher's *City* (1961), *Then Hallucinations: City II* (1962), and the eventual republication of *City* (1969) by Fulcrum Press. Even with Robinson's attentive introduction as a roadmap, *The Citizen and the Making of City* can present the reader with an embarrassment of riches. The overall effect of moving from one text to another is akin to Fisher's own experience of Birmingham's streets: it often feels 'impossible to trace the line of a single one of them by its lights'.

Yet when the author is as concerned with 'the physical presence of the city' as Fisher is, there is a certain joy to be found in being lost. Sketching Birmingham's urbanity with careful intensity, the city and its inhabitants are described in 'The Citizen' with such lavish bleakness it often borders on allegory. In section 6, for example, the city streets are populated with 'the dead black of the chimney breasts' and 'broken windows advancing'. Fisher's intimate familiarity with this material environment poses certain ethical questions about how, as people and bodies, we inhabit the city. In response, he is clear to outline his allegiance to the disenfranchised and vulnerable. In section 9 he writes that 'the governing authority is limited and mean' and positions himself against (or, at least, apart from) figures of supposed authority such as the police and 'the sensitive, the tasteful, the fashionable, the intolerant and powerful'.

This ethical positioning is complicated, however, by the 'detached' stance of the narrator as they watch and 'record' other individuals in the city. Such voyeuristic behaviour takes many forms here, from observing couples to effectively stalking a sex worker while she engages with potential clients. In section 24 the narrator relates – in almost obsessive detail – the experience of watching 'a quiet man of about forty in a loose raincoat' follow a lone woman as she leaves a pub. As he attempts, and fails, to proposition her, a policewoman quietly watches the exchange. In notes accompanying the text, Fisher recognises that 'this is terrible, in its values as well as its narrative', but that it has its place as 'the [voyeur's] point of view needs doing... *Everybody's* a voyeur at this time'. But these moments palpably breach the safety of the narrator's fellow 'citizens', and while these voyeuristic and often cruel moments would rarely find themselves salvaged or reworked into later publications, a certain disregard would still crop up in later works. In 'Lullaby and Exhortation for the Unwilling Hero', for example, Fisher writes: 'Pocket the key, and draw the curtains, / They'll not care.'

Simon Collings, who transcribed 'The Citizen' from its original notebook, remarks in the *Fortnightly Review* that Fisher's descriptions of voyeurism (and relationships more generally) are 'much softened in *City*'. Between this and Fisher's quiet lack of interest in revising or publishing 'The Citizen' in the following decades, it seems the author came to recognise the limitations of such a cruel mode – especially with regards to the vulnerable individuals he aligned himself with.

Yet there are moments in 'The Citizen' where the detached framework strikes through to remarkable insight and care, especially when contemplating the nature of gendered bodies and sexuality. In a section titled 'Under the Viaduct', the narrator describes a walk in the company of two sex workers they are vaguely familiar with. During this journey, the narrator reflects on how the sex workers offer an 'osmotic exchange of identities, sensations, attitudes', suggesting they will be 'freed from sexuality' – a change the narrator had often day-dreamed about. From within dissolution and exchange, a foundational empathy for one another can arise and allows us to orient ourselves to the shifting environments we inhabit. Through the text's concern with physical existence within the city and its lens of detached positioning, the narrator finds moments where traditional societal expectation can dissolve, and the role of 'the citizen' opens as a hopeful escape.

And as I take the 907 bus from Lower Bull Street back out toward Sutton Coldfield in the later months of 2022, I look across Birmingham's shifting horizon and easily recognise the same city that Roy Fisher was a citizen of. Even as I need to reorient myself to its turning pathways time and time again, this great wheel of a city remains, and we remain within it.

From the Archive

from *PNR* 170, Volume 32 Number 6, 2006

The Garpike

The garpike is an excellent table fish
I write these lines in praise of it although
There are some who would not, distrusting
Its mask which resembles that of an alligator,
And the bright green colour of its bones,
Which looks poisonous.
But in my south country childhood,
I grew to like the garpike -
There was a fisherman, who with his son, caught them
In Poole Harbour or maybe Christchurch,
And they would both arrive on a Friday or Thursday evening
With their catch.
And so I grew to value the garpike among other odd fish.

JOHN HEATH-STUBBS

more available at www.pnreview.co.uk

Some Contributors

Lutz Seiler grew up in East Germany but started publishing his poetry after the Fall of the Wall. He came to prominence with his first major collection *Pitch and Glint*, which will be published in English translation in 2023 by And Other Stories, at the same time the press publishes his second and prize-winning novel *Star 111* and *In Case of Loss*, a volume of selected non-fiction.

Oluwaseun Olayiwola is a poet, critic, and choreographer based in London. He's had work published in the *Poetry Review*, *Telegraph*, *14poems*, the *TLS*, and *bath magg.*

Sarah Mnatzaganian is an Anglo-Armenian poet. Her debut pamphlet, *Lemonade in the Armenian Quarter* (Against the Grain Press) won the 2022 Saboteur Award. Other poems have appeared in *The North*, *The Rialto*, *Poetry News*, *Poetry Wales*, *Poetry Ireland Review*, *Magma*, *Pennine Platform*, *London Grip*, *Atrium* and several anthologies. She won the Spelt nature poetry competition in 2021.

Maureen N. McLane is a poet, memoirist, critic and educator. Her latest book, *What You Want: poems*, is out from Penguin UK in June 2023. She teaches at New York University.

D.W. Brydon's poems have appeared in various magazines including *Agenda*, *PN Review*, *Stand* and *The London Magazine*.

Gareth Prior's most recent pamphlets are *The First Branch* (Contraband, 2021) and *Scattered Ashes* (Oystercatcher, 2020). He is Bursar and Fellow at St Hugh's College, Oxford, and a trustee of The Poetry Society.

Maitreyabandhu has written three books on Buddhism, three poetry pamphlets, and three full-length collections with Bloodaxe Books: *The Crumb Road* (2013, a PBS Recommendation), *Yarn* (2015) and *After Cézanne* (2019), an illustrated meditation. He was ordained into the Triratna Buddhist Order in 1990.

Judith Chernaik, founder of London's Poems on the Underground, is the author of *The Lyrics of Shelley* and *Schumann: The Faces & the Masks* (Faber 2018).

Kyle Lovell is a poet and the editor of Fathomsun Press. Their poems have been published in *Blackbox Manifold*, *Pamenar Press*, and *Ludd Gang*.

Rachel Mann is a priest and poet. Her debut Carcanet collection, *A Kingdom of Love*, was published in 2019.

Parwana Fayyaz is a scholar of classical and medieval Persian poetry, poet, and translator. Her debut collection, *Forty Names*, was published in 2021 by Carcanet Press, and it was named *A New Statesman Book of the Year* and a *White Review* Book of the Year.

Mark Haworth-Booth is an Honorary Research Fellow of the Victoria and Albert Museum. His latest book of poems is *The Thermobaric Playground* (Dempsey & Windle, 2022).

Nicola Healey's poems have appeared in *The Poetry Review*, *The London Magazine*, *Poetry Ireland Review*, *The Rialto*, and elsewhere. She is the author of *Dorothy Wordsworth and Hartley Coleridge: The Poetics of Relationship* (Palgrave Macmillan, 2012).

Maithreyi Karnoor is the author of the novel *Sylvia*. She is a Charles Wallace fellow in writing and translation, and a two-time finalist of the Montreal International Poetry Prize. She lives in Bangalore, India.

D.W. Brydon's poems have appeared in various magazines, including *Agenda*, *Stand* and *The London Magazine*.

Greg Thomas is a writer on art and literature based in Glasgow. He is the author of *Border Blurs: Concrete Poetry in England and Scotland* (2019).

Editors
Michael Schmidt
John McAuliffe

Editorial Manager
Andrew Latimer

Contributing Editors
Vahni Capildeo
Sasha Dugdale
Will Harris

Copyeditor
Maren Meinhardt

Designer
Andrew Latimer

Editorial address
The Editors at the address on the right. Manuscripts cannot be returned unless accompanied by a stamped addressed envelope or international reply coupon.

Trade distributors
NBN International

Represented by
Compass IPS Ltd

Copyright
© 2023 Poetry Nation Review
All rights reserved
ISBN 978-1-80017-369-9
ISBN 0144-7076

Subscriptions—6 issues
INDIVIDUAL–print and digital:
£45; abroad £65
INSTITUTIONS–print only:
£76; abroad £90
INSTITUTIONS–digital only:
from Exact Editions (https://shop.
exacteditions.com/gb/pn-review)
to: PN Review, Alliance House,
30 Cross Street, Manchester,
M2 7AQ, UK.

Supported by